The Coaches' Keys To

Client Creation

*How to fill your
coaching practice
with all the clients
you'll ever need*

REPHOEL WOLF

Copyright © 2019 by Rephoel Wolf

All rights reserved. No part of this book may be
reproduced or used in any manner without written
permission of the copyright owner except for the use
of quotations in a book review.
For more information contact:
Rephoel@RephoelWCoaching.com

First edition February 2019

Book design by Rephoel Wolf
Editing by Gitty Wolf
About the Author Photo Credit: Baila Rochel Leiner

ISBN: 9781798873250

To Gary Mahler for throwing me a buoy.

To David Schwediman for pulling me aboard.

To Steve Chandler for building the ship.

And to D.K. for throwing me into the water. Without you I wouldn't have met any the amazing people I just mentioned.

Acknowledgments

I would first and foremost like to acknowledge **Denise Mckinney,** who was my first ever success coach in the very start of my coaching journey. Denise brought this book to life. She helped me follow my 'inspired action', and lit the spark inside me that let this book come to life. I still can't believe it.

Gary Mahler, I have no words. The first ever supercoach to model pure Service. Finding me, making time for me, and changing my life.

Melissa Black Ford, a complete honor to have met you.

Dave, this is obvious.

Steve Chandler, for all I have reaped from you.

Rich Litvin, for the prosperous coach.

CONTENTS

Foreword..I

Introduction VII

1. The Big Secret...1

2. How To vs. Want To 6

3. The Therapist, The Friend, and The Coach.................12

4. So What Does A Coach Do?..22

5. Owners and Victims..27

6. Why Would Anyone Hire A Coach?.............................35

7. A Social Conversation vs. A Professional One 40

8. Getting The Word OUT...76

9. Free Sessions...49

10. Transformation vs. Information.................................55

11. Who Are Your People..62

12. Where Are Your People...68

13. Reaching All Those People...74

14. Inviting People Into Conversation 77

15. "Gosh I Gotta Talk To My Wife About This..."........82

16. ROI...86

17. Powerful Coaching..90

18. If You NEED A Client, You Need A Job....................99

19. Who Am I To Be Coach?..103

20.Serving Now...108

21.Refferals 112

22.Ditch Your Niche 119

23. How Quickly Can You Expect Results?................128

About The Author...136

Foreword

I never set out to become an author; it was never my intention. It was never my goal. I was happy for the people I knew who put out books, but in no way jealous. I was happy they had something to share with the world, something to put out there as their legacy. I never felt like I had any special secrets to reveal to the world and I was really okay with that.

I can't tell you exactly where the shift occurred, as I cannot tell you about the many shifts that occurred throughout my life, and especially my coaching life, but I can try. There was definitely a moment when it HIT me that every conversation I have with my clients and potential clients, everything I was helping them with and co-creating with them, WAS something I was sharing. It was some sort of me putting stuff out into the world. It wasn't NEW stuff. The world has been around for long enough that I can assure you there are really no ideas that are new and never thought of before. But that doesn't make it any less your own, or in this case, MY own.

It occurred to me that writing a book is not limited to those who will shatter the earth by storm with an idea that has never been revealed before. And even if it WAS only for those things, not every author can reach every person. Everyone has a different style. A different voice. And everyone needs to hear things in a way that speaks to them.

That's why I am ALLOWED to be a coach even though there are many, many superb and marvelous coaches out there, coaches that I cannot be mentioned in the same sentence as. Yet I am still a coach because I am needed for MY clients. My clients cannot be coached by anyone else if it is my coaching they are seeking.

With the help of my own coach, David Schwendiman, I realized that my voice, and my coaching, can help others through a book I write as well. I can't say ANYTHING I know or talk about originates at ALL from me, but at the same time, it really does. As I read from one of my favorite authors and mentors, Steve Chandler, when he was talking to a client and he said over a quote, the client responded "Wow, that was beautiful, did you make that up?" To which Steve responded "Yes, I just made that up from_____". Meaning to say, the idea originated from that person, and maybe these WERE his exact words, but each person processing ideas and quotes through their own mind and brain, applying it in their own context, makes it their own. And that makes it available to a whole new world of people, who couldn't have heard it any other way before.

That's when I realized I DID have what to share. That which I have coached my clients on and continue to do so on a daily basis. This is my voice. This is my coaching. This is my gift to the world.

*   *   *

I decided to focus my book, my gift to the world, around a problem I know I struggled with as a coach and that I constantly see other coaches and entrepreneurs struggling with. And that is the famous million dollar question: How do I get clients? This really is a million dollar question, no jokes, because as soon as we figure this out, there really is NOTHING holding us back from hitting those million dollars.

I'm really passionate about getting this out to people, because the reason I AM a coach is my deep rooted hate (which I

KNOW is a strong word) when I see people struggling. I hate it when people are stuck. I hate it when people aren't sharing with the world their own gifts and talents. I hate it when people short change themselves. And the fact that this is all cause by our own internal beliefs, our limiting beliefs and the way we see the world, drives me mad. Because that means that the answer is right there! It's in your reach! You are so close to what you want, all it takes is a shift in thinking. A challenge to a belief. A simple, deep, good look at yourself and the way you view the world. And the minute you change your beliefs, you change the WORLD as you know it. This is something fantastic authors before me have already written about, and which I will not attempt to summarize or replicate here. That is not the subject of this book. Or at least not completely. Yet it's a process to properly tackle this question and something that when I try to do with clients too fast, they miss it. It either becomes too much too fast or they miss the beautiful simplicity of it all. And they don't even realize they KNOW the answer, even when it's been presented to them.

For this reason I chose to write this book in simple chapters that are little ideas that can be implemented each on their own.

That can be easily chewed and digested, to allow the mind shift to occur naturally and gradually, to help YOU, like me, not even know WHERE the shifts suddenly occurred that made life so beautiful and different than how you saw it before. That way you will get maximum impact and it outlines it to be an easy task.

Without further ado, dive in dear reader, and it is my greatest hope and fervent prayer, that this book helps you along your path to prosperity and success, and helps YOU help your clients in the way that only YOU can.

Much love,

~ vi ~

Introduction

Getting clients, or 'Client Creation' as I like to call it, seems to be the biggest challenge facing coaches who are trying to make coaching a lucrative career. I know it was for me. I know it's what brought me to my amazing coach, Dave Schwendiman. And the more coaches I spoke to, the more it became clear that we were all running into the same problems. I found myself having the same exact conversation with coach after coach. Coming in with one set of beliefs of what needed to be done. Moving into what would happen if we dropped all that. And what happens when we open our minds to learning, and to keep learning, new ideas. And when we keep applying and trying new things through trial and error, and stay open to reinventing ourselves, results show up in our lives.

It doesn't have to be complicated. It doesn't have to take years and years of trainings. It's about tuning in to the most intuitional ideas that come up for you and applying them. And never giving up.

CHAPTER 1

The Big Secret

In order to address the right way- or maybe it would be better to say the more *effective* way- to getting clients, it is so crucial to first talk about what DOESN'T work. If we don't explore the myths we currently believe that are keeping us stuck, we won't even be able to HEAR the way that WOULD work, because our minds are not ready for that yet.

It brings to mind that which Steve Chandler says about "mindshift". When the mind is ready, it will shift. Like when you're driving a stick shift car and you're getting up on your gear there and the car starts whining, it means it's time to shift into a new gear and you can't shift until then.

Also, one of the things I learned from the health coaching school that I went to (which in and of itself left much to be desired, but there were some great points and this was one of them), is that in order to bring in some new ideas, we've got to get rid of the old ones first. You can't move in the brand new leather couch you bought before you first take out the old one. With our minds too, if we don't clear out the wrong or bad stuff, there is nowhere for the new stuff to even land.

So when I am speaking to someone and I can tell they are clearly not ready for big changes in their lives yet, and they say "So how do YOU get clients? What are YOU doing that's working?" I'm more than happy to have that conversation with them, but we first have to talk about where they ARE and what's NOT working for them. And these people get annoyed, as if I am steering the conversation AWAY from me and making it about THEM (which I AM doing-heck, I'm a coach! That's what I do!), when really, the only way for them to be READY to hear

THE COACHES' KEYS

what's working, is to clearly identify what's NOT working for them. Let's get RID of those things, and then we can start developing a new idea, or in this case, easing into what I would be proposing as a novel idea.

But there's no way to just JUMP into that. And I would LOVE to. But I'm telling you I have tried this more than once with prospects, rushing to what WOULD work when they were not ready yet, when they weren't willing to look at what they were doing that wasn't working, and it just flew right over their heads. It made no impact whatsoever. Because they were not in the right place. When someone doesn't slow down and take a look at what they are doing that they need to discard, they believe the most common myth.

This myth is: they think that all they are missing is that ONE piece of secret information that all successful people know that they never heard of yet, and if they gather enough from enough people, they are bound to come across it.

Truth is: They WILL. But they won't even see it. Because it's not really the information which is missing. It's the

REPHOEL WOLF

TRANSFORMATION. And I tell you it took me years to realize this. Literally years and years that I too was chasing this SECRET piece of information, this special well-kept secret of life, that if I only KNEW what it was, I would be happy and on top of the world. And finally I came to realize, through much trial and error, that there IS no secret.

If you were to read "The Prosperous Coach" by Steve Chandler and Rich Litvin, which I highly recommend as that is what started the change in my life, you will find a chapter called 'The secret is that there is no secret.' That, I'm sure you can imagine, is highlighted AND circled in my copy. And it's more than just information. Let that line sink in and TRANSFORM you're life. It's pure gold.

THERE IS NO SECRET.

So now that I've gotten you good and curious, though that was not the intention, we now know why it's so important to figure out what we are doing WRONG, get rid of that, and be

THE COACHES' KEYS

open to this mysterious secret that THERE IS NO SECRET.

CHAPTER 2

How To VS. Want To

A lot of people think that they are stuck at "How to do something." Most of you might have even picked up this book because you wanted to know "HOW to get clients." We think the only think we are missing is that one piece of information which will take us out of the stuck state we are currently at, and have everything fall into place. The only thing we need is just to uncover HOW to do it.

In the words of my mentor, Steve Chandler, (I can hear his voice in my ear right now from his many audios saying this), "Now that's not really true." We are NOT just missing the HOW

THE COACHES' KEYS

to. Let me give you an example.

Let's say there is a roomful of people who have come together to support each other and learn just HOW to lose weight. They think that that's all they need to know. They all want to lose weight, some even have very strict doctors' orders to lose weight fast, and they are all trying to figure out just HOW to do it.

Let me ask you something. If I offered $1 Million dollars to whoever lost the weight they needed to lose in the next 90 days, how many of those people do you think would take me up on that challenge? For a million dollars? Sure! All the hands in the room would go up. Everyone would MAKE SURE to lose the weight. There would be no question about it. And suddenly, everyone would have great ideas and plans to follow to make sure that happened. And get this! Each person would probably have their own UNIQUE way of losing the weight!

But how did that happen? I thought they came into this room not knowing how to do it? What suddenly shifted?

The WANT TO. The intention. They now REALLY want to lose the weight in a way that nothing was going to get in their

~ 7 ~

REPHOEL WOLF

way. Now they are committed.

So many times we make this confusion. What we think is a lack of knowledge of HOW, is really just a weak intention of WANT. When we focus the intensity of our intention to WHAT we want to do, all the 'how to' questions and doubts fall away. When the 'want to' is strong enough, we figure out how to. We'll call people, we'll do research, we'll come up with all kinds of creative ways of reaching our goals.

And this plays itself in so many different ways in our lives. I was just talking to a woman the other day who told me one of her biggest problems right now in her life is her health. She had a whole slew of health issues and hospitalizations and this that and the other thing. So I asked her what needs to happen to get her health in order? And she told me, she has to start eating the right things but she doesn't know what to eat! [Now, just so you know, I am no nutritionist or dietician, and even though I am a certified Health Coach, it means absolutely nothing, therefore I try not to tell people about that at all. And STILL, I gave her one of the best pieces of diet advice I have ever heard, that I even went afterwards and called my Mom who is a former Weight

~ 8 ~

Watchers Leader and told her this great strategy plan and she was impressed.]

So I asked this woman, what do you mean you don't know what to eat? So she says, her doctor said she can't have any of the foods she likes. None of them! So what should she eat? To which I replied, do you mean to tell me your doctor only told you what NOT to eat but he didn't tell you what you CAN eat? So she says Oh no, he told me I can eat this that and the other thing, but nothing I love to eat. So I don't know what to eat.

And I found it fascinating that she kept repeating she doesn't know WHAT to eat, when really she knew perfectly well what to eat! She just wasn't happy with her options and chose NOT to listen! That's what she told me. In other words, she didn't WANT TO. When I pointed that out to her that she knows exactly what she needs to do and what she can't do, she said yeah well then it gets too stressful for me and I eat everything anyways, and it's going to kill me.

Here I was fascinated once again. She knew WHAT she needed to do, she knew the consequences of her current actions, and she still felt like she didn't know what to do! So I decided to

~ 9 ~

try my best here. I told her, here's what I see. You can't eat the things you like. You know the foods you're not allowed to have are going to kill you. And yet you can't completely cancel them out because the pressure causes you to go all out and eat them always! So, why don't we try baby steps, like you tell your clients? (She was trying to be a health coach, if you can imagine.) Your doctor wants you to go from 0 to 60 (0 being always eating those things, and 60 being never) and instead you're going haywire! Why not make this sustainable and go from 0 to 1 to 2 to 3 to 4? Why not just commit to one day a week for now that you will not eat those things? To which she immediately said because I'm NEVER allowed to have those things! I shouldn't EVER have them. To which I said but you are anyways! (Laughter). The word SHOULD just traps us, limits us and make us feel bad and build up pressure. Making changes comes from CHOOSING to be different and creating a sustainable plan. To which she agreed.

My point in this story is that the 'how to' works two ways. Sometimes we think we only need to know HOW to do something when really we just have to turn up our WANT to.

THE COACHES' KEYS

But it also works when we don't WANT to do something, we'll just say that we don't know HOW to. Which in essence ends up being the same thing.

Which is what Steve Chandler says over in the story (in his book 'The Story of You) that at a writer's seminar he attended, the leader responded to the question "What do you do when you just don't have time to write?" with the answer "You don't have time to write because you don't WANT to." Simple as that. When you WANT something, you make it happen. You figure it out. If something is not happening, it's because you don't want it to.

So if you wanted to be very blunt with someone, which is totally your choice to use whenever you'd like, if someone ever tells you I just don't know HOW to do this! I don't know how to make more money. I don't know how to take care of my kids. I don't know how to make my wife happy (which is indeed a tricky one), you can calmly respond, on the contrary, you simply don't WANT to. And you will be correct.

So if you very simply wanted to know "How do I get clients?" The answer is: You WANT to.

~ 11 ~

CHAPTER 3

The Therapist, The Friend, and The Coach

When it comes to getting clients as a coach, it's really important to be clear on what it is you do, and whether people know that or not. I'm not sure if you ever wondered this before, or if you only thought about it after people have confronted you, ever so rudely, but what DOES a coach do? WHO needs a coach? Is a coach just someone who you are paying to be your friend? If you have a good enough friend, can she be your coach and you're good to go? Is a coach a watered down therapist? Or worse, is he an ILLEGAL therapist who is practicing therapy without a license?

THE COACHES' KEYS

I'll have you know that there are more than a few insecure therapists who view coaches like that. I have spoken to some of them personally. They think either people who need a therapist are cheaping their way out of therapy by going to a coach. (Which obviously can't mean monetarily cheaping their way out because a coach can charge significantly more than a therapist if he or she wishes to do so.) Or they think that the coach is trying to cheap HIS way out of all the years of school needed to BE a therapist and is trying to pass himself off as an expert without any of the necessary schooling. Which is so ludicrous for a therapist , who is a mental health professional, to be so insecure about what THEY do, and not see that a coach is so different and is in no competition with them at all.

This question is so important to know the answer to, and once you do, you will see no question in the first place.

I would like to give you some of my own personal background, which has led ME to this question, and I will tell you how it resolved itself.

The first coach I ever saw in my life actually presented himself as a kind of therapist. He actually introduced me to what

~ 13 ~

a coach is, after I had gotten to know him and I realized there was work I myself wanted to do with him. And the whole time we worked together, I wasn't sure if I was seeing a coach or a therapist, so I just assumed either they were the same thing OR he was BOTH. Either way, it worked for me and I loved the work we did together. And honestly, I told my close friends I was seeing a therapist because I *wanted* him to be a therapist, I was not afraid at that point of sharing that I was doing deep work on myself, and I loved it. So having a therapist was a great pride for me. Although looking back, he really was just a coach practicing some therapy techniques, which I have no issue with and I loved that, but really truly, it's not the job of the coach to do with me some of the things we did do together.

But the point is, it was from that experience that I was indeed confused about what the difference between a coach and a therapist was. And so, when I came to the point in my life where I knew coaching was for me, and I set out to find a life coaching course to qualify myself- for as every beginner coach believes, that is what you need to get started- I decided to ask the organizations I was talking to about this factor. If they could

THE COACHES' KEYS

help me understand this difference, and then help me out with that into the world, I would be on the right track and I would know which to choose. (Because there are SO many people trying to sell you their certifications before you find out you don't need any of them, the choices can be overwhelming.)

The first people I called, and ended up going with, told me very simply and clearly (and kindly I should add) that therapy digs really deeply into old wounds. Coaching doesn't really dig so deep. We don't try to figure out the underlying wound behind the issues that are showing up. We just figure out ways to deal with the things we don't want NOW, and make new habits around that.

I think that's all I heard at the time, and that sat really well for me. Because although from my own "therapist"/life coach, I learned HOW to do that, dig deep into the feelings and uncover all sorts of gooey stuff- and I liked it and was good at it too- I didn't WANT to be messing with peoples brains (too much). I didn't want to be responsible for helping them dig a hole AND have to figure out how to get them out as well. Because, as many of you know by now I'm sure, it's the job of the PERSON to get

~ 15 ~

REPHOEL WOLF

themselves unstuck, and what if they just couldn't? What was I supposed to do? And then I could get sued and blah blah blah, all those nightmarish thoughts.

So I was happy to hear that I was not going to be messing with brains.

It was interesting to note that the second place I called, just to have two options in front of me, actually got a little defensive. When I asked them "What's the difference between coaching and therapy?" they quite curtly , and annoyingly (which are obviously my judgment and not clear fact) said, "You better know the difference between coaching and therapy if you want to come to our school."

Now really? What kind of answer was that? So not only did you not answer my question, and if I hadn't already known, you have left me in the dark, but you were rude about it too, so of course I will not be attending your school. So I went with the first one.

NORMALLY I would say it's the insecure therapists who get defensive and upset at coaches for 1) stealing business from them and 2) for pretending they are therapists when they are

~ 16 ~

THE COACHES' KEYS

NOT! Here I found some coaches getting defensive as well, apparently.

(On that note, I actually saw a therapist write an article once, titled "Life coaching? Not on your life!" and proceeded to write a very accurate article about what a therapist does and how a life coach does not and should not be doing therapy. The article was very agreeable. So I couldn't figure out why she thought a coach WAS a therapist. AND she ended the article with: "Any coaches out there who want to say something about this are welcome to respond." So I sent her an email, being very polite and respectful, that I completely agree with her article, and that coaches indeed DON'T do what therapists do. And, I am not sure how, but she published my letter as a follow up to hers, and somehow tried making me look like the idiot she was painting coaches out to be. And she ended THAT response with her title, "So like I said, 'Life coaching? Not on your life!'" And I really think she just made herself look very foolish with that.)

So that's our first clue: Coaches don't dig deep into emotional past and therapists do.

But just because one school said that, doesn't make it the

~ 17 ~

most accurate. But as far as my journey went, I was starting to see what my job would be and what MY first coach did that was considered therapy. Again, I personally loved him for it and I love the work we did together, but just getting clear on the difference.

You know, it's coming up for me right now a little meme a friend once sent me when he heard I was a coach. It happens to be I thought it was hilarious, but it goes to show the worlds confusion of what a coach is. It read:

"Stop being an a******.

There.

Now I'm your life coach."

It's funny because I just think it's funny. BUT what we do see is that people think a coach is someone who just tells you what to do or how to act. That's not it.

What I WILL tell you though, and I honestly only realized this now, is that there IS a very important key here to what coaching really IS about. When you stop to think about it, how many people will actually tell you, seriously, to stop being an a******? Honestly. Not many.

THE COACHES' KEYS

Why? Because it's not very nice. So either they like you too much to insult you that way. Or they care about hurting your feelings or the relationship between you. Or because they really don't like you, so they are just being mean and trying to get you upset.

BUT a coach WOULD tell you that. Why? Because a coach is NOT your regular buddy buddy friend. Friends like each other, support each other, and want to keep the relationship. Even if they are sometimes blunt with each other, they are not as completely devoted to the other person's personal growth as they are to maintaining the friendship.

A coach is so much more than that. A coach is committed to the same things YOU are committed to. A coach will tell you what you NEED to hear, not what you WANT to hear, regardless of how you'll think of him afterwards.

I once told someone, if you don't ever not like me enough when I'm coaching you, it means I'm not doing a good job. (It doesn't really have to be so black and white, but it's what he needed to hear in the moment.) Why? Because it's going to happen that you WON'T like what your coach is saying, yet you

~ 19 ~

KNOW he's right and it's the best thing for you. He's pushing your buttons because THAT'S where you need to go. Doesn't mean you'll like hearing it.

When people don't want to understand what the point of a coach is, they will say "sounds like a friend who charges you. What if I have a good enough friend, and he won't charge me, why waste money on a coach?" First of all like we said, a coach is NOT a friend who charges, a coach is telling you all the things that your friend WILL NOT say because it's not socially acceptable for friends to say that. But more importantly, you are not paying the coach for his time, for his hours. A coach is not CHARGING you. When you invest in a coach, you are investing in YOURSELF. You are committing YOURSELF to getting the results you want in your life, and you are investing in the coach to help you get there.

Every professional, the more professional they are or want to become, has a coach. Coaching comes from the world of sports. No athlete, actor, or singer goes without a multitude of coaches.

Getting a coach is a sign of commitment to success.

THE COACHES' KEYS

Whatever you want ENOUGH in your life, you get yourself a coach to help you get there.

No friend will ever be that committed to your success, because 1) they have a life of their own, and they cannot give complete focus to your goals and progress. But 2) because you are not investing in YOURSELF, you won't always listen to your friend even if he DID do everything a coach would do. Because he's just your friend after all and if you want you can listen, and if you want, you can just as easily ignore him.

This is why I have a coach. And HE has a coach. And HIS coach has a coach! Sounds like a cult? Maybe. But we are all achieving in our lives what we couldn't do otherwise. And loving everything about it.

CHAPTER 4

So what DOES a coach do?

So what IS the clear defining line between a coach and a therapist? Can it be summarized in one simple, easy to say over line?

YES.

As I heard from my mentor Steve Chandler SO BEAUTIFULLY on his audio titled "Why would I hire a coach?", which is serious recommended listening, the most over simplified way of putting it is: "Therapy is about the past, and Coaching is about the future."

Therapy is about healing past wounds. Figuring out where

THE COACHES' KEYS

they crop up in present day life. Look at problems, find the root, figure out what caused it and work on a slow healing process of the past. TREMENDOUSLY useful work, and definitely has its place. It's just not right for everyone, and definitely not the only answer to most problems.

Coaching is about CREATING the future. Coaching is about figuring out what the clients' future WOULD look like, if they could design it any way they wanted. If they could be who they WANTED to be, as opposed to what they think they MUST be from past limiting beliefs. And then *going* there. Sometimes all it takes is *living* from that place as if it were true NOW. There are many ways of shedding limiting beliefs. But therapy doesn't have to be the only answer.

Therapy is so useful, and sometime *crucial*, and if you have all the time in the world, and not enough motivation to make changes NOW, I would tell you to try it out if you think you need it. (Many have reported that they needed a coach in ADDITION to their therapist, so they were working on two playing fields at once. That also makes perfect sense to me.) But if you want results in your life right NOW, coaching is the way

REPHOEL WOLF

to go.

Forget about WHY you have this limitation or WHERE it comes from. You have the ability to choose right NOW. What do you want? Regardless of the past, what do you want to create for your future? What do you want to create right NOW? Your past is a place of reference not a place of living.

Coaching has a sense of urgency to it. People can be in therapy for YEARS and come out the same way as they went in. For they aren't creating a future. They are healing a past. Necessary, no doubt. But doesn't mean they'll have a better future. They need help CREATING that. A therapist's job is not to create. They MAY help you do that as well. But that's not their job. Their job is to charge you X amount of dollars for an hour a week of exploring the past. Whether that changes your life is not their business. As always it is up to you, the client, to make that change. To take what you are learning and discovering and figuring out for yourself what you want to do with that.

But the coach's job is to help you live better NOW. Help you create the future you only dreamed of. Help you make it a reality. ALSO through your own commitment, but he will see

~ 24 ~

THE COACHES' KEYS

that you are sticking to it. And if you are not, he will catch you on that too.

When I was speaking to a potential client, I realized the first two times we spoke, she was venting to me like she vents to her friends. She wanted me to side with her like her friends do. She was already seeing a therapist, yet she was still as stuck as ever- which just goes to show how much therapy was doing for her. When I stopped her in middle of her rant and said 'What would you like to CREATE? You don't need me to agree with you like all your friends do. You have them to side with you and agree that your life is terrible. That's not what you need me for. What DO you want?"

I knew, and it might be obvious to you as well by now, that it would be no service to her to keep letting her tell me how terribly unfair her life is and how she is a victim of circumstance. Either she wants to stay there and there's not much I can do for her anyways. Or she wants to take control and figure out how to make something work. But complaining, take it to your friends. Not a complete stranger who is here to help people change their lives and take empowered action. I am here

REPHOEL WOLF

to help you take OWNERSHIP of your life and actions. Not to allow you to stay a VICTIM of circumstance.

CHAPTER 5

Owners and Victims

In case you have never heard of those two words before, or that context, I will try my best to clarify it for you. Just so you have fair warning, Steve Chandler has dedicated an entire book to the owner/ victim distinction. It is called "Re-inventing Yourself" and it is amazing. He also has an audio titled "The Owner Victim Choice", which I'd be happy to send you if you shoot me an email, Rephoel@rephoelwcoaching.com. And Dusan Djukich, in his super powerful and amazing book "Straight Line Leadership", has a chapter on the Owner vs. The Victim, which is probably where I have learnt about it so well

~ 27 ~

REPHOEL WOLF

myself.

Anyways, after that introduction, the only real way to describe the Owner and the Victim is by comparing and contrasting.

The Victim REACTS to things. The Owner CREATES things. (Did you know that REACTING and CREATING have the same letters? It's up to YOU how you want to arrange them.)

The Victim can't do anything about the situation. The Owner can ONLY do. (Which is why a coach cannot help someone who wants to STAY a victim, because they are not willing to make anything happen in their lives. They are a victim of circumstances. However, the victim might still go to a therapist and the therapist will happily listen to the victim victimize for an hour, and maybe that venting is healing for the client. But it's not what I do as a coach.)

Victims CAN'T and Owners CAN. You'll hear this in the language they choose to use. (A person's use of language is so key and essential to who they are, you can learn A TON about people's lives from just noticing their choice of words.)

Victims have dreams. Owners have projects.

~ 28 ~

THE COACHES' KEYS

Victims are SURVIVING. Owners are LIVING.

Victims will always use words like "Should".

"I really should clean up around here."

"I should exercise more."

"I know I really should... "

Should just puts us down. It makes us feel shameful for what we are NOT doing. It's NEVER a way to motivate oneself.

Owners WILL do something. They make up their minds. They either decide I WILL clean up right now or I WILL NOT and be happy with that. They are making a clear DECISION what they will or will not do.

Victims TRY.

"Will you be there on time?" "I'll try."

"Can you clean up this house before bed?" "I'll try."

They spend a lot of time TRYING, which is a non-committal way of saying "I'm not going to commit myself to making sure it gets done." As opposed to saying "Yes" or "No." Would you lend someone 10k if he says he will TRY to pay you back? No. You wouldn't lend him ANY money. You want to know he WILL pay you back.

~ 29 ~

REPHOEL WOLF

An owner WILL do it. He will CHOOSE. He will be clear and concise in his commitments. "Yes, I WILL be there on time. I WILL pay you back. I WILL clean up this house." Or he might choose NOT to, but he is CHOOSING.

To a Victim, it's just how things are. To an Owner, anything is possible.

The gist of it is, that it's a place of BEING. A place to come from. To a Victim, there's not much that can be done, and there is no responsibility for making anything happen. They really truly are just 'victims of circumstance'. Their life is glum, trudging through tasks, trying to 'make it through the day.' Wondering when this life will finally be over.

To an Owner, life is exciting! Unlimited possibility! Something is wrong, let's make it right! Let's create! Let's get whatever is in the way OUT of the way! I'm not surviving! I'm loving life! I love being responsible to make things happen, and if nothing is happening or flowing into my life, I know it's because of me and let me see what I can do to make that change! If I make *myself* into the problem, then I can find a solution.

To a Victim, OTHER PEOPLE are usually the problem, and

~ 30 ~

THE COACHES' KEYS

there is nothing I can do until that person changes.

An Owner recognizes whenever there is something in his life he doesn't like, he makes himself into the problem so that he is free to create a solution.

So if you are talking to someone and they can't see out of the box that they've trapped themselves in, and they are not willing to look beyond that, then what CAN you do for them? You can bring the horse to the water, but you can't force it to drink. (I am so sorry for bringing in such a cliché line, but I really really had to. I CHOSE to;-)

I want to end off though with a fascinating story that JUST happened with me yesterday (from the time of writing this), that I THOUGHT was a contradiction to what I just told you, and my coach helped me see why it was not so.

I was talking to a client of mine who had bought my starter package, (a shorter term package to start the work together and get a feel if it's something they would want to continue for a longer period of time) and we were discussing continuing. From our work together, my client kept on using victim language and seemed unwilling to take ownership of what he COULD do and

~ 31 ~

REPHOEL WOLF

CREATE in his life. He was very set on his "personality type". (Which is victim thinking. Our personalities are just stories we tell ourselves about who we are, but are not essentially in our DNA). And why his personality type has to do things a certain way and no other way works. To me, though he was HAPPY being that way, I saw it as complicating his life and really getting in his way of what he wanted to create. After sharing my thoughts with him, and even explaining the owner victim distinction, he patiently explained to me again why I just wasn't getting it, and he IS a certain type, and he knows it's a small box, and he wanted help FITTING and STAYING in that box! My head was spinning, I'll admit.

He basically was telling me, at least this is what I heard, is that he wants help STAYING a victim! Was that something I could do? I help people take OWNERSHIP! I help people get OUT of that! How do I LET him do that?

As I thought, I asked him how he wanted me to help him stick to his personality type if I don't understand it nor do I believe in it? And he said, exactly like we've been doing until now. You keeping me accountable and keep having these

~ 32 ~

THE COACHES' KEYS

conversations like we've been having. That helps me.

Well, THAT I could do. But more than that, I also realized something.

I, as a coach, am here to help people get to where they want to get to. I keep on saying that I have no personal agenda. So how can I now go and say, "I will not help you be where you are happy being and WANT to be, because it's not what I would prefer?" That would be against everything I believe in.

Because that's just it. I DON'T know what each person needs unless they tell me. If someone has a list of limitations they would LIKE to live in, and they have guidelines for me how to help them do it, then THAT is the service of this person! That's what THIS person needs.

My coach helped me realize that we ALL have our own limitations we make for ourselves, our own decisions on how we decide to live. Doesn't make them BAD or WRONG, it's just how we are CHOOSING to live. If we choose to live our lives with our own rules and boundaries, which we have a right to do, than our coach will help us WITHIN how we choose to live, to get to where we want to go, even if he has none of those same

~ 33 ~

REPHOEL WOLF

limitations.

It's when the client is UNHAPPY with their confines and feels stuck there, that unless they are willing to look outside of that, we cannot help them. If the client has a victim attitude and the world is a cruel unhappy place and they wish it was otherwise, yet they don't want to be open to something else, what can you do for them?

But if, like my client said, he WANTS to live by how the book says his personality is, and he wants to work WITHIN that, they key here is that he IS willing to work, and he knows HOW he wants that to be, and he is WILLING to make it happen like that.

That, in truth, is not a victim at all. That is the owner spirit showing up in its own unique way.

CHAPTER 6

Why would anyone hire a coach?

For a lot of new coaches out there, as passionate as they are about what they do and what they want to get into full time, they run into a simple and common question. And if you haven't pondered this question, it's actually a GREAT question to ask yourself, in your quest for client creation.

"WHY would someone hire me to be their coach? How do I turn these people who I am always helping ANYWAYS into someone that I am actually coaching?"

This is a great question, but it begs for deeper exploration into the world of what coaching really IS and why indeed

REPHOEL WOLF

anyone should want to hire you for that.

You see, a lot of coaches on the outset discover their passion for coaching when they notice how much they LOVE helping people. How fulfilling it is to be the person who people approach for advice, and how to really create change for that person. To help get them on the right track. To help them see outside themselves, for we cannot see the rut we are stuck in because we are so close to it.

But that's just it. I have had coaches come to me and tell me people are always coming to them for advice, and to unload. And to have this coach, being such a wonderful and listening person, give them advice and make them feel better.

But that's NOT what we are doing as coaches. We are NOT advice giving or making people feel better. We are activators of personal change. We help people see where they are stuck BECAUSE they CAN'T see, for they are so close to it. We are NOT givers of advice. It could be we ARE good at giving it, and it IS helpful. But that's not WHO we are.

We help draw it out of people themselves. Help THEM figure out their own answers. It will only work if it comes from

~ 36 ~

THE COACHES' KEYS

them.

This is why EVERYONE can ALWAYS benefit from a coach, no matter who they are or how old they are. No one is too good for a coach. A person is like a jar with a label. NO ONE can read their own label! A coach is simply the eyes on the outside, who can see what we can't possibly, and who is not caught up in all the emotion WE are which most of the time is what keeps us stuck.

How ironic is it that a coach would tell me that she was super stuck and not doing well and her husband says, "Why don't you coach yourself through your own program!" And she thought what a great idea! And she proceeded to do so! So she was excitingly telling me how she was really happy to be able to share this own personal struggle with her clients, to show them if she could do it, they could do it to. Well, what I heard from her is that the same way SHE apparently didn't need a coach to help her, her clients don't either need her. Why would her clients pay her to help them, when it's apparently something you could do by yourself? Yeah, they MIGHT want to pay her because she has already gone through it, but why can't they find

~ 37 ~

REPHOEL WOLF

the same people in the world who have gone through it and not have to pay, just like SHE did? Do you see what I saw there? It's very very silly from the outsider's view in my opinion.

A coach is a co-creator. We are creating together WITH the client what is needed for THEIR life. For their best life. What would help them if they didn't want to keep going along their default life?

And some people WANT to stay in their default life. They don't WANT to take responsibility for their life's outcome. It IS a lot of work, I won't deny it. And not everyone is ready for that.

Which is why coaching is not for everyone. You can't just get up and start coaching whoever you meet, or even those people who come to you, because they do want change, until you know they are really ready to commit to it.

So the difference between those people you are already 'helping' and 'giving advice to' is that those people are not looking for major change in their lives. The biggest proof is because they keep on coming back to you! They are committed to making anything HAPPEN in their lives.

They feel good after they speak to you, they seem real

THE COACHES' KEYS

happy and thankful and love your ideas, but they haven't changed. It feels good to think you have helped them from that encounter which is why you keep doing it, but you're not doing what you REALLY want.

If you REALY want to help people, if you really want to give people results in their lives, you would be coaching them. You would make it into a professional conversation. You'd turn it from being a social, friendly, supportive chit-chat into a life changing talk. How?

Simple. Read On.

CHAPTER 7

A Social Conversation

vs.

A Professional one

How do you turn a regular social conversation into a professional coaching conversation, which will have the person react to it differently? It takes a simple, but powerful mind shift. And that is: WHAT are you doing? WHO are you when you're doing it?

Are you a nice friendly person giving friendly advice and emotional support to whoever needs it? If you are, that's

THE COACHES' KEYS

amazing and super kind of you and fills the world with a lot of good stuff.

BUT.

You cannot charge for that. OF COURSE people will run away from you if you suddenly tell them 'Yeah, this thing that we do all the time when you come to me for advice? I'm going to start having to charge you for that. Yeah, sorry. It's just that I got bills to pay. Maybe when I make it big we can go back to how we've been doing it until now.'

What you ARE doing, if you want to be a coach is *really* helping people. Give them results in their lives. Help them CHANGE so they won't be this sad victim-like person always needing a pick me up. TEACH them how to pick themselves up. DRAW it out of them.

COMMIT to them getting *lasting results* in their lives.

That's entirely different from what you've been doing for them until now.

Until now, there ARE things you've been holding back from saying because it's not sociably acceptable. You don't want to hurt their feelings. You don't want to look like a bad guy. You

~ 41 ~

don't want to look dumb.

When you're a coach, it's not about YOU! It's about THEM. The only way to make it about them is to be committed to THEM by telling them what they NEED to hear not what they WANT to hear. The only way for you to be fully committed to them, is for them to be fully committed to you. The only way they will commit to you, to commit to lasting change in their life, is if they hire you. (It is true, and I have fallen into this myself, that it's possible you will be committed to them even before they hire you, because you care so much about them getting unstuck. But what I want to watch out for is to make sure I am not caring more about them getting unstuck then they do.)

The next time someone comes to you, even someone who has been venting to you weekly, stop them. (Unless it's someone that you value your friendship more than anything in the world and it really GIVES you energy to just be there for them and do the same sympathetic nod every week.)

When they say they want to talk, when they say they need advice, stop them right there. Tell them you'd be happy to help them and talk to them. Tell them you do this professionally, and

THE COACHES' KEYS

you'd be happy to make time for them, but it's going to have to be a set time, and you can make it up on the spot together, but we aren't going to have a deep conversation on the fly like this. Your time is too valuable AND it will not be helpful to them.

Person: "Hey Rephoel! Gosh I really need to talk with you, things are just going crazy right now and I really need some advice...."

Me (having heard this one before): "Oh really? Sounds crazy. I would love to talk with you and see what we come up with as this is actually what I do all day. Why don't we pull out our calendars and see when we can soonest find a time? I have tomorrow or early next week. How does that sound?"

Do you see what I've done? I've turned this from being a social conversation to a professional one. Professional doesn't mean I am charging for it, as a lot of coaches make that mistake. I CAN'T charge him for anything yet, as I haven't shown what he would be getting yet. I don't KNOW what he would be getting because we haven't talked and I don't know what results he is after, if there are any.

But I have made it professional by saying 'Let's make time

~ 43 ~

to talk about this.' Making time is the first step to making a commitment to one's self.

I actually just got off the phone with someone in middle of writing this chapter who said he wanted help making more money, but he has no skills or professional background. So I simply asked him "What do you LIKE to do? What makes you come alive?" As in the famous quote from Harold Thurman Whitman, "Don't ask yourself what the world needs. Ask yourself what makes you come alive and then go do it. Because what the world needs is people who have come alive." I knew if he figured out what makes him come alive, we could make that into something lucrative for him.

And he says, "I actually don't know. I'm always looking for that thing to make that fire inside me light up but I need to make time to think about it." I told him "Well, now's your time. You take it as much as you want, but now we're on the phone and you've made the time for yourself, so think about it. There's no rush." And he says, "I need to take much more time than that; I couldn't do it on the phone with you." So I said okay great, so what are you going to do? So he said he will have to make time

THE COACHES' KEYS

to think about it. So I said, well what makes you think you'll do it now if you haven't done it until this point in the past? And he said, you're right. And I said, you have to commit to setting aside that time and making it happen. Because I can't really help you, if you have no idea what you want to make happen and you have no plan to make that time for yourself. To which he agreed, and I made him, on the phone, take out his calendar and tell me what time he is setting aside for that.

Once you have set up the time to talk and let them know this will be serious, they will take it more seriously. They will suddenly get alert. They might even say 'No I don't need that I just need to quickly...' and you'll stop them. You don't have time and energy to waste on them right now when they clearly don't want things to be different. When they want things to be different they will set up a time. And sometimes, even then, they are not going to be committing to making any changes, but at least YOU have set up the conversation in a way that would be most helpful to them. And that's what we want, after all, isn't it?

~ 45 ~

CHAPTER 8

Getting the Word OUT

How do you get the word out? How do you let people know that you do this coaching thing? Most people would tell you that you have to advertise. Consistently. For a long time. Is that really true? Can you absolutely know that that's true? For those of you who don't know, those two questions are the first two in Byron Katie's Four Question mind blowing life changing formula that will turn your life around. (The name of her book is 'Loving What Is'. Go read it). But it really is a good question. Who said you need to advertise? What does advertising do for you? Now I don't want you to say 'Everyone says you gotta

THE COACHES' KEYS

advertise; it's the only way to get your name out there.' Because first of all, who is 'Everyone'? The advertising agency? The paper? The radio? And second of all, you don't need to get your name OUT. You need to get clients IN. No matter how many times people hear your name, or see your smiling face, that will not cause them to work with you. Nope. It won't even cause them to give you a call to check you out. Why? Well why WOULD it? What makes you different then the thousands of other people ALSO just trying to 'get the word out'?

You know what the answer is? You know what makes you different? I want you to think about that for a minute. Go on. Stop reading and think. What makes YOU and YOUR service different, and BETTER, than anyone else out there that people should pay you any attention? Write it down.

So now that you're back, read out loud the one word you just wrote. You didn't write more than one word, did you? Well, I apologize if I just wasted your time and ink on that one, but you SHOULD have only written one word. And that one word is: YOU. (Or you probably wrote "Me.")

YOU are what makes you different. YOU are what makes

~ 47 ~

your service better. NO ONE in the world can bring into the world what YOU can.

And how do your ads convey YOU? How will people know who YOU are from seeing your face, or seeing what your job is, or from hearing your name?

THEY WON'T.

We don't need to get the word OUT. We need to get people in. The way to get people IN, is to GIVE them YOU already. Start giving people YOU. Let them EXPERIENCE YOU so that they can say 'yes' to working with you. Give people the EXPERIENCE of you so they can tell all their friends and family about you as well. Your raving fans are your best advertisers. (Read the Book 'Raving Fans' as well.) Stop advertising. Stop getting the word out. Start getting people IN.

THE COACHES' KEYS

CHAPTER 9

Free Sessions

I'm all for helping people already before asking for payment. In fact, I encourage you to focus all your efforts on that. That's the focus of this book. Serve first. Everything else will follow. Give people YOU so they WANT to hire you and want to come to you.

What we want to look at here is that which people are so fond of GIFTING sessions, or giving away FREE service. Putting yourself out there with a gleam in your eye, an overly genuine smile, saying "I will give you a FREE session. I am giving FREE consultations, or FREE business advice- no commitment

~ 49 ~

necessary. Those are all things which tell the person you are talking to, that you are about to rope them into a conversation which will end in a proposal and they will feel obligated to make an awkward excuse. When you use the word FREE, it means you have an agenda. Besides for the mantra circulating in the world 'nothing is free', which might be true, it just SOUNDS like you are up to something. *Especially* if you preface it with what you are doing for a profession.

You: "Hey I'm a life coach! I could help YOU with your life! I'd be happy to give you a free session!"

Person you're talking to: "Thanks! But I'm good! I actually don't have anything in my life I need help with!"

I have never taken someone up on an offer when they offer to talk to me for FREE. Ugh! It just feels so gross and I *know* something is up.

But what's so beautiful about examining what *not* to do, it really shows us what we *can* be doing. When you know which ingredients to omit, you are left with fewer options about what *should* be going into the recipe. In this case it is so so simple to turn it around. Because like we said, helping people for free is a great thing. It won't get them long term results possibly, but I'm all for serving people before they even *know* who we are. I will *show* them who I am *by example*.

So in this case, all I have to do is *omit* the word FREE. That's it. Here's what that would sound like.

Me: "Hey, so I heard you saying you were struggling with XYZ. I help people with that all the time and I'd be happy to sit down and have a talk with you about that, if you think that would be helpful."

Person I'm talking to: "Wow! Really? That would be amazing! Thank you so much!"

The only people who are going to be suspicious about talking to you when you offer just to have a talk with them, are people who you probably *can't* help right now, and who you probably don't want to have to deal with anyways . However, when you are offering FREE stuff, you are turning away even the most wonderful prospects.

A lot of coaches struggle with the big battle of charging for initial sessions. There are two sides. If you haven't caught on by now, I highly disagree with charging for initial sessions. What

REPHOEL WOLF

exactly are you charging FOR? An hour of your time? Is that all your service is? It's a time based service? Are you a house cleaner? Or a babysitter? If you ARE, then OF COURSE you charge for the first hour you work with someone, for that hour is no different than any other hour you would be working with them.

But if you are a SERVICE provider, be it a coach, an insurance broker, or real estate agent, you are not charging for your TIME. You are charging for what your client is GETTING. For the results they will HAVE. That is not an hourly charge. It's how much this result is worth to this client.

If that is the case, it makes no sense to charge them before they have EVER spoken to you. They have no idea if you can help them! YOU have no idea if you can help them! You have no idea if they can be helped or NEED anything in their lives right now! So I HAVE to have an initial conversation with them to know if this can even be a fit!

But more than that. Even if you DO have a great initial session, they might still not know what this will do for their lives until they go away from the conversation and think about what

~ 52 ~

THE COACHES' KEYS

you discussed. Apply what they've learnt, if they've learnt anything new. Let them see how they can take this first conversation into their lives and decide if they need more of this.

So charging for the first session, besides making no sense, are you really provide X amount of dollars of value to your client in this one conversation alone? Are you really?

And I want to say, even if you DO get someone to agree to pay for the initial session, you are taking a HUGE risk. They might NOT get any value from the conversation and resent you for wasting their money. They might GET value from your conversations, but decide that they don't need this long term so not sign up with you, and then the value seeps away pretty fast, as life continues on more than your short livid inspirational conversation can provide. And then they will look back to you as someone who took their money, costs money to ever talk to again, and tell their friends to stay away from you.

People want to send their friends to people they like, know, and trust. And just HAVING that first conversation with no agenda, no proposal, and no sale, just SERVING, will build that

~ 53 ~

REPHOEL WOLF

up so fast for you, you will be getting referrals left and right.

THE COACHES' KEYS

CHAPTER 10

Transformation Vs. Information

A common objection I get, and I have heard people passing around, when I introduce this idea to people of serving first, is "But you can't give your stuff away from free! Then they won't hire me to work with them! They'll just take what I give them and run!"

First of all, I really want to honor this concern and I hear where they are coming from. I'm sure I believed that at one point as well. I can't say for sure, because honestly as soon as I learned about this idea of service, I was totally on board with it, it really made a lot of sense to me, and I know a lot of people

~ 55 ~

REPHOEL WOLF

that take years to adjust to this concept. So lots of respect there.

Secondly, I do want to say that I too was originally coached this way that you don't want to give away TOO MUCH for free for that exact reason; if you give it all away they will see no reason to hire you.

So what I want to bring up over here, that in all honesty, if ALL that people were missing was some INFORMATION, then they really DON'T need to hire you. And if they really *wanted* that information, they could find it all on Google. You can find *anything* you want to know on Google. How to play the piano, how to write a book, how to paint, and even how to TRAIN YOUR DRAGON!! (I just typed "How to... in my google search box and that's the first thing that came up. You should totally try it yourself and see what happens.)

We know that the people who need our help, the people we WANT to help, are not just missing information. That's not what we are offering. We are not just offering information. If we WERE, then I have to admit, you're in a tough business, because why SHOULD anyone pay you for your information if it IS all available somewhere out there in the world?

~ 56 ~

THE COACHES' KEYS

I was actually talking to a coach the other day who was trained in a certain, very scripted, program to lead clients through. She wasn't loving it but didn't know what else to do. So I asked her, "What would you do if you had NO information to give your clients? What would you do?" She said "I'd probably just coach them where they are at." BINGO.

That's ALL you need to be doing. Another coach I was talking to, who was stuck in all her own problems in her life, thought she needed to do her training all over again because she forgot most of what she had learned during very turbulent times in her life. And I asked her, "How do you know you can help people at all?" To which she responded "Because I've been helping people for years even before my training and they got great results!" And I showed her what she just told me. She just told me she helped people WITHOUT any new information, yet now she was stuck thinking she couldn't help people unless she knew more. She laughed when I pointed that out to her.

If we too believe all we are doing is giving information, then we will feel that struggle of helping people before they hire us.

But that's NOT what most of us are doing. No matter how

~ 57 ~

REPHOEL WOLF

much INFORMATION we give people, what they are missing is TRANSFORMATION. As the saying goes, 'It's not WHAT you know; it's who you are BEING."

Steve Chandler has a great audio titled 'Information vs. Transformation' and that's what it's about. No matter how much we help people, and really SERVE them, their lives won't really change until they TRANSFORM. And most people need to commit to the work to experience real transformation.

I was speaking with a woman, let's call her Stacey, who was clearly not into the transformation stuff. She was just looking, looking, looking for more and more information to solve all the problems in her life. I was guilty too, by the way, of always looking for "the book" I may be missing, but I realized long ago, there IS no "book of secret answer". One of the greatest chapter titles in the Prosperous Coach book (amazing book by the way, go read it) is titled "The secret is that there is no secret". But this woman was still there. Where's the book that will help me parent better? Where's the article that will solve my child's tantrums? Where's the book that will teach my kids to sleep at night? She actually told me that she DID cave in and hire a

~ 58 ~

THE COACHES' KEYS

sleeping coach, who would coach you on how to get your kids sleeping through the night and into routine. The key to it working is consistency. She offered 8 sessions, and while it was hard, and wasn't perfect, this woman saw results. When the 8 sessions were over and she felt she had enough to go on with and not continue for longer, the coach suggested a book on sleep training for further issues or things that might come up.

Stacey reported to me how upset she was. This book said EXACTLY what the coach had told her to do- her whole process! "I could've just gotten this book to start with and I would have saved hundreds of dollars!"

No Stacey, you couldn't have. Because it's not about the INFORMATION. It's about the TRANSFORMATION. The book is a nice tool, but it won't make you use it. You won't commit yourself to the book. The book won't make YOU transform. YOU make you transform. When YOU committed to the coach, you were committing to YOURSELF. You were committing to get your money's worth by doing whatever it takes. THAT'S the point.

But Stacey didn't want to hear of it. Her belief that coaches

~ 59 ~

REPHOEL WOLF

were just highway robbers was ever deepened.

AND when she *was* not consistent with her children's bed schedules, she lost all the progress she gained and was stuck almost exactly where she started before she met the coach. Which I am sure you can imagine made her very upset. At the coach.

And then, when she was finally fed up again, she says "I wonder if that coach has another book on sleep training that would help my *current* situation, as it's very different then it was before, and the previous program will not work anymore."

No Stacey. Even if she *did* know another book, it wouldn't help you. But you don't want to see that.

That's why it should be our PLEASURE to give things away to people for free. Give and give and give them! It MIGHT help. It might inspire. It might get them thinking. But the real change comes from their commitment and investment.

Even if people say they *have* been changed from our conversation with them, and they don't need anything else, that's GREAT! That's what we want to do! Change people's lives for the better.

~ 60 ~

THE COACHES' KEYS

Now they MOST probably will need us again in the future, as life keeps on going, and even if this thing is fixed, there will be others that come up. And now they know where to go to get that fixed as well. Now they KNOW what it's like to work with us, and somewhere down the road they WILL come back to us. What a beautiful seed we have planted, putting that service into the world which WILL come back to us, one way or another, for every seed planted in the universe grows under the right conditions. When you take care of people in the Universe, the Universe takes care of you.

So go ahead and give out whatever it is that will serve the person in front of you. I promise you, you can't lose.

CHAPTER 11

Who Are YOUR people?

I would like to share with you one of the most amazing questions I know of. I'm not sure if I totally invented this myself or my brain picked it up somewhere when I wasn't looking. But it will have such a profound impact on your business and client intake, you won't remember what life was like beforehand. However, the first question we need to look at, before the earthshattering one, is "Who are your ideal clients? Who are you looking for? Who, when you see them, do you KNOW you can help? Who are those people that you would LOVE to cross paths with?"

THE COACHES' KEYS

Now, I'm not asking you for your NICHE. If you have been trained in finding a niche and getting super clear on EXACTLY which 12 people in the world you coach or serve, *please* do not think about that right now. That's your own business that I am not talking about. I don't want you to think of niche. Niche is an extremely limiting thing, a belief a lot of us have been trained in and bought into, and will have you going around saying "I coach rodeo clowns. If you are not a rodeo clown, I'm probably not the right fit for you. I can TRY but really I only coach rodeo clowns." No. that's not what I want you to think about. I want you to think about which people are you looking to help? What problems do they have? What are things they say that when you hear it you go "Oh! I can help them! They need my help! Why should they be stuck there?" The problems people have that EXCITE you because you know you can change their lives? Who are they? What are they saying? What do you see?

Once you have figured that out, not only will you realize that that is WHY you decided your 'niche' was rodeo clowns, you will see that a vast amount of people who are NOT rodeo clowns *also* have those problems and obstacles and can equally

~ 63 ~

REPHOEL WOLF

use your help. [So why limit yourself? I'll tell you what you were probably told in just a moment.]

Now we come to the life changing question: Do those people KNOW they need your help? Do they KNOW they are stuck? Are they actively looking for a solution? Or have they accepted this as just the way of life? If they are not looking, how will they find you? If they don't think they need help, how will seeing your ad, or watching your video, bring them into your world?

I don't know about you, but I'll tell you what I was taught. I was taught that the reason that it's SO important to have a niche is, because if you don't, you're just another 'coach' in the world. How on earth will they find YOU? You have to have a real specific niche so that the person who fits that exact mold will kind of gravitate towards you (somehow). I was taught that it is likened to a hallway lined with doors, and every door has a nameplate on it. You want the name plate on your door to be really specific, like 'I help rodeo clowns feel really happy day in day out without tiring, losing energy, or getting sick of horses', so that WHEN the rodeo clown with that problem is walking

~ 64 ~

THE COACHES' KEYS

down the hallway, he MIGHT decide to go into the door that says 'LIFECOACH' or 'Anti-Depressant Doctor', but when he sees your door, he will fill with joy, burst through the door in excitement and say 'Please work with me!' without having ever even spoken to you! Because of your Niche specific door!

Wouldn't that just be amazing? Aren't we all just excited for such a great fantasy? I will admit, I bought into it as well, so I'm not mocking. Until I am.

That's just ridiculous. You CAN still believe this, and I give you full rights to laugh in my face and tell me that's EXACTLY what's happening in YOUR life, and I'm just jealous. BUT then why are you here? I'm writing this book for people who want to know what works. There can be thousands of things that work in the world, and if your world already looks like that, that's fantastic! There's really no reason for you to be reading this then!

BUT, for all those of you who HAVE tried that without amazing results, or never even tried because it just sounded too crazy, let's talk about why that might be.

The reason is because people are NOT looking for their

~ 65 ~

problems to be solved. Most people don't even realize they HAVE them. Most people accept their unhappiness and unfulfilled lives as what life IS. Even if it's obvious to you and me, they have no clue. They are too close to the problem. We all are too close to our own problems, and that's why it's so important for EVERYONE to have someone looking at them from the outside, telling them what they see, and helping them grow to be bigger and better people. It's why I have a coach. And he has a coach. And HE has a coach. And my life has never been better.

But if people don't know, they are not looking. It's all a myth. There is no hallway. There are no people walking down the hallway. And even if there WAS a hallway and there WERE people, there are no doors. There is no place where every person is listed with exactly what they do that anyone who wanted help could scroll through.

If that's the case, well then THIS is why we struggle getting clients. We sit by our desks and phones and emails, waiting for people to find us and contact us, when really just the opposite should be happening. We need to be out there finding THEM.

THE COACHES' KEYS

We need to be out there looking for people with problems we can solve, and offering them to fix it. We need to show people what life could be like other than the default life they are now living. The only life they know of.

We shouldn't be sitting, like victims, waiting for the world to respond to us and bring us clients, and if not, we must just 'not be cut out for this business'. We need to be ACTIVELY CREATING clients. Getting clients IN and not getting the word OUT. Getting the word OUT will do NOTHING if people don't know why they need to be IN. People can see your name and watch your videos, but not know what this has to do with them.

And even when you FIND those people and offer to help them, you think you can radically change their life in one sit down meeting which will have them hire you on the spot? But let's get to that later.

~ 67 ~

CHAPTER 12

Where are my people?

Even once we get the idea that there are problems to solve EVERYWHERE around us, we just have to tune into our daily conversations to notice them, sometimes things feel slow. Or they DO slow down. Or we don't get out much. Where are we going to find people to help? How do we find those people? Where am I going to go once I really have my intention tuned up and I'm ready to save the world?

I just had this the other day. The way it played so perfect, it was as if it was scripted. I was speaking to a client, let's call him Rob, who wanted to transition into coaching, and was talking to

THE COACHES' KEYS

me about what that might look like.

One of the things I love to ask people and help them get really clear on is "What is this transition going to give you? What are you looking for more in this other venture in your life that you don't already have?" Besides for this being just a great question, it also helps really strengthen and up the WANT here, so that the person is ready and willing to make anything happen.

So Rob says, "I'm always helping people, people are always coming to me for advice. I really connect with helping people, and I really want to start doing this professionally."

Okay, cool, sounds like a great place to start, with some minor mindshifts, but that's not for now. When I helped him shift out of what he believed was 'just giving advice to friends' into a professional coach who helps people get amazing results in their lives he said, "Oh wow. Yeah so I gotta look outside my circle of friends who are already coming to me and set up other relationships like you're explaining to me." And I said, "No, Rob. I need to stop that thought in its tracks. That is exactly wrong. It's NORMAL to think that. I used to think that too. A LOT of coaches STILL think that, but it is incorrect. And I will save you

~ 69 ~

REPHOEL WOLF

a lot of wasted time RIGHT NOW. Let me give you an illustration." I told Rob to listen or draw this out if he was a visual learner, and I said "Imagine you draw a circle in middle of a blank piece of paper. This circle is YOU."

"Now draw a circle around that one. This circle is the people closest to you, who know you the best. Like your friends and family. Draw another circle around that one. These are the people slightly more removed from you, people who only know you through your family and friends. Keep drawing more and more circles, around and around.

THE COACHES' KEYS

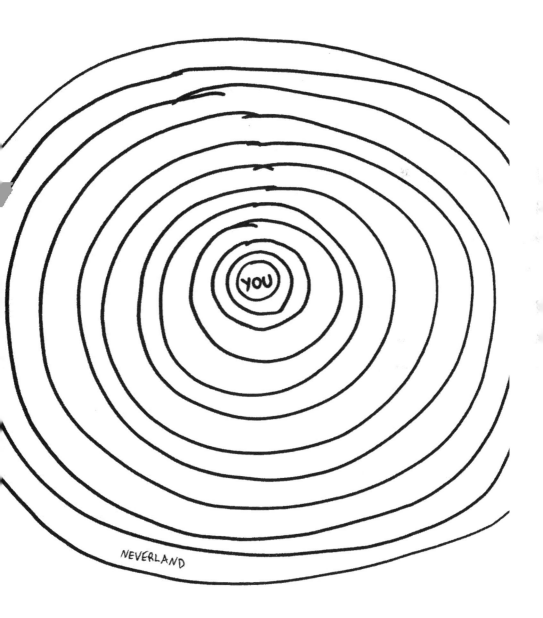

REPHOEL WOLF

The further the circle is from YOU the less connected to you they are.

Most people and coaches try right away shooting for the 16th circle, people way out in the world they don't know. Sending little video clips into the internet for someone to chance upon. Just setting up a website for someone to find by mistake. [I actually saw a coach who had an introduction video on her website that started off with "Hi! I'm___. And I am SO happy you found me!" Like straight out of a fairy tale! You FOUND me, and now I can change YOUR life!

This is a mistake. It's not effective. And it doesn't make much sense when you sit and think about it for a second. The TRUTH is that your key to steady clients is THROUGH your innermost circle.

BESIDES for the fact that you can help those people who you are already helping, that you can turn those friendly chit chats into real lasting results for those you care most about, they are your key to the world beyond.

The people who know you and like you and are familiar with your work are your greatest assets. They will be the people

THE COACHES' KEYS

who are going to tell people about you, refer people to you, and simply rave about you. (Read the book Raving Fans by Ken Blanchard. THAT'S the gist of the book). Those people who are ALREADY experiencing you, or who will most willingly talk to you already, are the people you should be helping/talking to first. They are the first circle.

You need not look past your contact list, or the emails in your inbox to find a whole list of people you can help. Reach out to them. Check up on them. Let them tell you where they are at. Listen to their answers. Find those problems to solve in their replies or their unspoken replies. And offer them to fix it.

CHAPTER 13

Reaching ALL those people

A lot of times, we as coaches overwhelm ourselves. The truth is, in many professions they do this. They go out into the world looking for ALL those people they can help. All those people who could use their services. They panic in overwhelm. For sure in big networking groups (a sad waste of time in and of itself), "How will I have enough time for everyone should know who I am and what I do? I better host a talk! I better make an event that's focused on ME!

But then what will I do? How will I follow up with each person! I can't do this all by myself! I better hire a team! And a marketing director! And a campaign manager! And get myself licensed bonded and insured! And, and , and.....!"

Slow down. Can you just breathe for a minute? Calm down. Focus. Stop.

You don't need to reach *all those* people. You don't need *everyone* to have your business card. You just need to find the *one* person, the ONLY person RIGHT NOW, that you can help.

When I used to go to networking events and I had learned about this mind shift, I practiced this. I would go in looking to find the ONE person I was meant to meet. The ONE person I can help. All it takes is one person. One meaningful connection. I can only work with one client at a time.

Even if I were to be putting together a group program, the focus is not 'Where do I find the people to fill my group with?' The focus is 'Who can I add to my group RIGHT NOW? Where is the ONE person who could benefit from this?'

And then I find the next ONE person. I am constantly only focusing on the one person in front of me right now. That's where mastery comes in.

I am modeling for my clients how a focused clear slowed

~ 75 ~

REPHOEL WOLF

down life looks like.

When I go out into the world looking for ALL THOSE clients, my task becomes overwhelming. I start to lose myself. I stop seeing who I am with because I am thinking of all the people I STILL need to meet and find.

And therefore everyone gets nothing. They get none of me, because I am somewhere else, and I get none of them because they feel I am not connecting with them.

Connection is the key to conversation. Conversation is the key to a client. Clients are the key to a prosperous practice.

So slow down, realizing that here, as in many other cases, LESS is MORE. Find that one person. Serve your butt off. Then find the next one and repeat.

CHAPTER 14

Inviting people into conversation

Okay, so now we know that people are rarely looking for us. And we need to bring ourselves to them and bring them in. We are on the lookout for clues for problems that we can solve. We go out into the world. What do you see? What do you hear? How do you know when you can help someone? What are they saying? Be like Sherlock Holmes. Looking for mysteries to solve and solving them no matter what. He does not get tied up into how he looks and who is he to solve this problem. He doesn't even CARE about the PERSON he is working with, rather the PROBLEM that needs to be solved. OF COURSE, we CARE

~ 77 ~

REPHOEL WOLF

about people, that's why we are in the business we are in, but this is not about US. Not about our credentials, or how we are coming across, or if we sound professional enough. We just know we can help, and we go in to help.

When You DO hear or see something that makes the bell go off in your head –"*Ding! Ding! Ding!*"- Now what do you do?

You do what you are best at. You start TALKING to them. Engage them in conversation. LET them talk to you and tell you what's going on. Sometimes we approach people in conversation with our professional front up and we preface with "Hey I'm a life coach/business coach, and I can help you.....". That could be innocent enough, and you can be honestly just trying to engage them in conversation and assure them you are a good person to help them. But that's not what they hear. THEY hear "I'm probably going to ask you to hire me in the most immediate future."

Prefacing with WHO YOU ARE means you are focusing on yourself and not on them or their problem. And they will sense it. Not to say this is set in stone and never works, and that there may be people so wrapped up in their problem they will talk to

THE COACHES' KEYS

ANYBODY so they're not listening to your language so much, but we want to set ourselves up so we can help as many people as possible, and if it's right- to hire us. So we want to LET PEOPLE talk to us, and take as many possible obstacles out of the way.

So the BEST and EASIEST way to do this is just forget about WHO you are, and tell them HOW and WHAT you can help them with.

Example:

Bummed out dude: "Man, I wish I could bring in some more money. But I don't have any college degree, or crazy new product to introduce to the market! I don't know WHAT I can do!!" (This has really happened to me.)

Me: Hey, I actually help people make more money without either of those things. Would you like to make a time to talk about that? Would that be helpful to you?

Dude (not bummed anymore): Are you for real?? That would be sweet!

It makes such a difference. I can't describe it- you just have to try it for yourself. And I didn't struggle for too long as I had a

REPHOEL WOLF

coach guiding me the whole time, but this is something I learned. I couldn't figure out why a lot of the time I was being met with resistance to my innocent offers to help people and my coach told me this secret. A person's guard is *always* up when being approached by strangers, or even friends who are "offering them something". But for sure when you preface with your profession, it means this is about to be about your profession and probably a sale in there somewhere.

If we just drop that language, and continue the same exact way, it has such a different effect. We want to minimize resistance as much as possible. So do whatever you can that allows people to let you in to start helping them.

After that it's only a matter of time for them to decide if they want to CONTINUE working with you, or if they really have been so helped by your one conversation, that they are good for now. For as Steve Chandler says, "No one was ever hired outside a conversation. Every sale happens in a conversation."

No one should ever have to decide to START working with you. The question should always be do they want to

THE COACHES' KEYS

CONTINUE? And you have to aid them to getting there.

CHAPTER 15

"Gosh, I gotta talk to my wife about this."

Money Objections. Our clients usually have them. And honestly, we all have some of them ourselves. On the one hand, we understand our client's objections. Maybe they really DONT have the money. Or so it seems on paper when we help them calculate their expenses. On the other hand, we know they WANT what we have to offer, they've TOLD us so ; we know how all their money problems would go away if they worked with us. So what do we do?

I think the first thing to look at, is where are there money beliefs living inside OURSELVES? Are WE, on some level, not

THE COACHES' KEYS

willing to invest in something that would drastically invest in our lives, and therefore we can sympathize with the client, because we are holding onto the same thoughts? Are we allowing them to fall into their story, because we are falling into a similar one ourselves?

If that is so, how can we POSSIBLY tell them to invest in us, when we don't believe in investing in ourselves? That would be like going to a doctor to write us a prescription and the doctor says 'I personally don't go to a doctor or take prescriptions, doctors don't really know what they are doing and drugs are a deadly thing, but what can I write this out to you for?' That's EXACTLY what it is like.

After we've looked at that, let's look at the objection for what it really is. They say they can't afford it. It's too expensive. They REALLY REALLY need this in their lives, they just can't make it happen. Ok. Challenge: Is that REALLY true? If there WAS something you needed more than anything in your life, would you not be able to figure it out how to make it happen? We can look at this in two ways, either positively or negatively.

Let's start with the positive. If I would pay you $1 Million

~ 83 ~

dollars to come up with X Amount of dollars that you just told me you can't afford, in 30 days, would you take me up on that challenge? Would you? There's not one person who would say no. But how would you do it?? When the incentive is high enough, you figure it out.

And on the negative side. If you were to DIE if you didn't come up with the money in 30 days, would you be able to come up with it? I bet you would.

And that's because when the drive is high enough, we make things happen. We create the money. We'll sell everything we own for $1 a piece until we had enough dollars. We'd ask anyone we could think of to give us a donation to change our lives. We'd make a lemonade stand for 5 cents a cup. There are things to do. We just have to WANT to do them.

If we buy into our clients' money objections, we are not serving them. We are not being a coach. If they say ' I can't' they mean, 'I'm not committed to. I am not invested in this. This is not important to me.' And if they had just told us a minute before how much they need this, how much they want this in their lives, then when they bring up a money objection, there's a contradiction right there.

It's probably our fault. We probably didn't adequately show them what they could be getting by working with us and how majorly this can impact their lives. We might not be the right person for them. It might also be that now is NOT the right time for them even if there is nothing else in the way. When they want it enough, they'll have the money. When WE want something enough, we know we'll figure out how to make it happen. Let's show our clients the same thing as well.

CHAPTER 16

ROI

What is an ROI and why do you need one? Well, ROI stands for Return On Investment. It's the REASON people are going to be paying to work with you. When you are talking with someone about hiring you, when you are talking to someone about your services, you (maybe unknowingly) are showing them the return on their investment. What will they be GETTING from working with you? Why is your service crucial to their lives? What will this DO for them? That's what an ROI is, and why it is SO crucial to the success of your business and people hiring you.

THE COACHES' KEYS

Very simply, because if there IS no ROI, then why WOULD someone hire you? Obviously if you HAVE a business, if you are looking to help people with whatever your service does for them, then your service DOES do something for them, we don't have to explain that much. We need to be showing them what we are offering which is the reason they are going to shell out all this money for our work.

The thing a lot of service providers, and specifically coaches run into, is that they are not showing a REAL ROI. They are offering SOMETHING, but the potential client is not really sure what it is.

An ROI has GOT to be something concrete. It has to be something tangible. Something they can see and feel and post about on FaceBook.

Increased confidence is not an ROI. More fulfilling relationships, is not an ROI. More energy and direction in your life, is not an ROI.

What's funny is that I too learned this the hard way. I was presenting such vague, coachy sounding stuff, that SOUND nice, people nodded thoughtfully at them, but it didn't bring me any

~ 87 ~

clients.

Me: If you were to work with me, you'd have more confidence. You wouldn't care what people thought about you and you would suddenly see how free you could be in your own life.

Their thoughts: Wow I'd love to have more confidence. That would be useful, somewhere down the road. You know what? As soon as I pay off my credit card debt, finish up my mortgage, upgrade the house, send all the kids off to college- oh, gosh, I need new jeans-, as soon as I do all THOSE things, you know what I'm going to do? I'm going to hire this guy and invest in this coaching.

So basically, they will hire you for those intangible things when they have more time then they know what to do with, more money than they can handle. Which is when they are DEAD essentially. It's like, the moment before death you'll get that call, and then death.

If we want people to work with us, if we truly want to HELP people, we have got to show them an ROI that's real.

If I know when I work with people, they will have more

THE COACHES' KEYS

confidence, what does THAT do for their life? How will this newfound confidence AFFECT them? I want to look at what my coaching does to the grand scheme of their lives and present them with THAT.

I'm offering the same thing, but I'm presenting it in a way that's real and tangible and in a way they can hear it. In a way that allows them to really see what working with me will do for their lives, and allows them to say yes to the work together.

People who are more confident lead better. They ask for more. They make bolder propositions. If someone is looking for a promotion or a raise, it will be really hard if they are lacking in confidence and self-worth. If we were to work together, those things would fall away, and there would be nothing stopping them from asking for- and getting- that raise. Their own self-worth would radiate and they would know they deserve it.

So instead of me telling them 'You'll have more confidence', which as of now they aren't really connected with the fact that they seriously LACK in confidence, it would be "Our work together would get you a promotion/ more money (raise.)" THAT'S an ROI.

~ 89 ~

REPHOEL WOLF

And again, the work is the same. What I'm offering is the same. But by changing my language into a way that makes SENSE to them, I am making it easier for them to get into the work together.

And now when I see coaches/professionals making these videos, and saying really passionately 'I can help YOU transform YOUR life, so you will be living your true energetic purpose', I'm just dumbfounded. That literally means zero to me as a viewer. It only tells me that they are struggling with their business, because that's just not going to work.

So get your ROI nice and clear, and you won't have to have client fear.

CHAPTER 17

Powerful Coaching

Maybe you've read in some coaching books about this idea of 'Powerful Coaching'. I have to be honest with you that when I read about coaches having powerful coaching conversations, or hearing other coaches talk about the powerful conversations they were having with clients, I was intimidated. And I felt dumb. "Are my sessions powerful? Is there some sort of powerful information I don't have that I'm not bringing to my clients? What does this MEAN?"

This was back in my days of still believing all the noise people are making in the world about themselves, and still

REPHOEL WOLF

doubting (clearly) if I had what it took to really coach powerfully, and if maybe I couldn't make it in this profession after all.

I love my coaching. I love helping people. But what's this 'POWERFUL' stuff they speak of, and how do I get it?

I ALMOST fell into the trap of maybe I DO have to go to all these seminars out there to really GET it, and THEN I will be up there with the pros.

If you have ever felt, or still do feel, the same way, I'm happy to bring this to you. As we talk about in the chapter Transformation vs. Information, coaching is NOT about the information you are bringing. It's NOT about what you have to offer. It's about the client's TRANSFORMATION. That's what they are paying you for. That is what you are helping them with. THAT is where you are guiding them.

You don't need to know ANYTHING in order to do that. Other them to SERVE them, right NOW, in THIS moment. With no agenda in mind other than 'What does this client NEED'?

THAT is powerful coaching.

~ 92 ~

THE COACHES' KEYS

Coaches sometimes get mixed up and they say they are setting up 'Powerful Coaching Conversations'. A powerful coaching conversation is when the CLIENT has a major breakthrough, which only can happen IN the conversation. So how can you possibly set that up BEFORE the session happens??

When I go in TRYING to make it powerful, when I go in just brimming with ideas and trying to MAKE something happens, it usually backfires. Besides that I am going to blow them away, and come off too strong, I am focusing too much on myself. I'm making it about ME then, about how good I am and what I can BRING, as opposed to being focused on THEM and what THEY need. As soon as the focus turns away from them and onto me, I've lost them.

Maybe they don't need ANYTHING? Maybe they just need to TALK and be HEARD and then everything will fall into place by them? Maybe when I sit silently and hold their space, they will come out so clear- and think that I've done it for them!- that I need not share ANYTHING of my own!

I found this time and time again, and I've read about it too but I never really GOT it until I tried it, that the POWERFUL

~ 93 ~

moments in my coaching session happened when I was SILENT. When the client says something, or even when I've said something, and there is really nothing more that needs to be said, and I HOLD the silence. Let it stand. Let things sink in. My most powerful times have been then, when I let the silence reign. When it feels awkward and I continue to hold until they continue. It's almost counter intuitive yet it is so very effective.

Silence will trump information almost EVERY TIME! Check it out for yourself. Instead of needing to fill the space and MAKE it powerful, let it just BE. Let thinks turn over in their brains. Let them tell you what needs to happen.

I was once reading a newsletter from Rich Litvin, and he wrote about this one time his coach served him so powerfully. He said that he had been procrastinating writing an article and he was really getting stuck. When he got on the phone for his session with his coach, who at the time was Michael Neil, Michael said "Well then, write right now. No more putting it off. I want you to write it while I am on the phone with you. I'll put myself on mute and you tell me when you're done." And he spent the whole hour on the phone with his coach, silently

THE COACHES' KEYS

writing the writing he had been pushing off, and he got it done. Fifty five minutes later he said, "I'm done." Michael responded, "Good call. Speak to you next week!" And that was it!

When I first read this, I was horrified! I was angry! I thought that was scandalous! THIS is what his coach took money for? And Rich is publicizing this story as if he was PROUD and APPROVED of it! What a sick coaching world this was turning out to be!

This was early on in my career. It took me a while to really GET what was happening in this story, and why Rich was happy about it.

What happened here was pure service. What happened here was powerful coaching. Michael knew that this writing was something that Rich had to get done. He also knew that Rich wasn't doing it. And he knew that if Rich DID it, it would move him forward. AND, what was very powerful is that Michael DIDN'T CARE what Rich would think of him for suggesting that he do it on the phone right now! Michael told Rich what he saw Rich needed to do.

What a powerful coaching move! To serve your client and

~ 95 ~

tell them what they NEED to hear, regardless of what they WANT to hear or what they will think of you! And Rich knew that as well! Which is why he was so happy and proud about this story.

Powerful coaching and powerful service. One and the same.

I will admit that this story gave ME courage, when I finally GOT it, that I probably would not have come to by myself for many extra years, even if I HAD fully understood service. This story so clearly and powerfully illustrated that, that now ANYTHING was an option. There was now NOTHING I could say to my client, that would be in service to them, that I needed to feel dumb about.

So when the time came for me to serve my client this way, I was able to confidently do so.

My client kept putting off an email we decided he would benefit from writing. All through the week he kept sending me updates that he didn't do it but he was going to do it. Tomorrow. Tomorrow. Tonight.

I had no idea what this email was going to be about or why it was important, but we had discussed that it WAS important

THE COACHES' KEYS

and that he would benefit from writing things out.

When our next session came, and he had still not done it, I coached him on that. I asked him what's going on. He admitted that it was just too painful for him. (Earlier in the week he told me he was embarrassed, and I assured him I did not need to see it and that it was purely for his benefit to get things clearly out on paper. Now the real reason came out.) He said he just needs more time for things to settle.

I asked him what will change if he waited and he said he needed to wait till it 'felt' better.

And I challenged him. I told him it seems like this is a really big block in his life, and until he writes this out, he won't be able to move forward. (And I didn't even know why but I saw how much importance he was giving it, and all the other things going on in his life, that it made sense to me.) I said, as your coach I am here to help you get unstuck. And this email is keeping you stuck. You need to write that email. And you need to write it now, while I'm here on the phone with you. You don't have to read it aloud, but do it right now.

And he did. It didn't take long. It took 10 maybe 15 minutes.

~ 97 ~

REPHOEL WOLF

And it was such a breakthrough for him. He said "I didn't even realize I FELT this way about these things!"

That was powerful. That was gutsy of me also. But I wasn't worried about him thinking I was wasting his time. I knew this is what he needed. I had permission from those greater than me to exhibit my service in the craziest ways. And I saw firsthand how much my client gained from me serving them with what THEY needed, and not with ME having to MAKE something powerful happen. That's powerful service.

CHAPTER 18

If you NEED a client, then you need a job

This happens to us, at all stages, all the time, depending on our mood, but sometimes we find ourselves with no one to help. No one to serve. And on top of that, there's a leak in the kitchen that needs fixing. And funds are low. And the spouse is driving us crazy to go get a real job already so we can have a steady predictable income. It won't be MUCH, but it will be steady. And predictable.

And then you find someone you CAN help. And you're bringing that pressured energy into your conversation. I don't know if you get where this is going, but this is NOT going to

~ 99 ~

REPHOEL WOLF

work.

You cannot be powerful coach if you NEED the client. First of all, you DON'T. If you were in service to them, you would only be serving them as much as they would find helpful. There is no YOU in this picture. It's only about THEM. Or at least, that's how it's supposed to be. As soon as you make it about YOU needing THEM, you've lost them.

Second of all, needy is CREEPY. They are going to FEEL your urgency to get them to work with you and it's going to push them away.

I want to make sure when I'm with someone, there is nothing on my mind other than "What can I do for this person" and "How can I fully be here and listen to them?" As Agnes Martin said "The worst thing you can think about when you're working with someone is YOURSELF."

This pressure you are carrying around with you is not only chasing people away, it's hypocritical. You are telling people you can help them and make their lives better, yet you clearly are falling apart yourself. Who wants to work with someone like that?

~ 100 ~

THE COACHES' KEYS

You may ask "But it's true! I need to bring money in from this coaching already or I'm done for! I need to pay the bills!" That's a great concern. So *figure out how to pay your bills without making that other people's problem.*

There are plenty of ways to make that happen. If you want to keep coaching, you cannot make your clients responsible for paying your bills. It's counter intuitive but the more you chase your clients to hire you, the faster they will run away. The more you are just present to them and put your worries away, and help them without thinking at ALL about the money, the sooner they will be running to hire you.

If you NEED a client, you need a job. Find a job to do on the side. Find a job to do 6 days a week so that you can focus all your love of service on that one day a week when you will truly be serving people. OR commit to coaching no matter what it takes. Offer people to coach them for a year for $1,000. Offer people to solve the biggest problem in their life right NOW for $100. Offer people $10 sessions! Coaches have done all these things, and have had success with them. The possibilities are endless. It all depends on how much you really want this.

~ 101 ~

REPHOEL WOLF

There's nothing wrong with bringing in income other ways until you can make your coaching alone lucrative. It's responsible. It shows your commitment to making coaching prosperous. But don't bring it into your conversations with people. Leave them at home with your spouse and the leak in the ceiling.

THE COACHES' KEYS

CHAPTER 19

Who Am I To Be A Coach?

Undoubtedly, the thoughts creep up sometimes, that we as the coach maybe don't know what we're doing. Can I really help ANYONE? Do I really have the answers to all their problems? Am I really able to help them accomplish things that I myself have never done? What if they find me out? Will I be sued? What if I DON'T know what I'm talking about and just make it up as I go along? Can you get a bigger fraud then that?

Well, just to answer those questions and doubts, I must ask you: ARE you an answer giver? Is it your RESPONSIBILTY to have answers to their questions?

~ 103 ~

REPHOEL WOLF

The answer is "No." If you are a coach and you're reading this, I assume you know how to coach but in case your approach has been different, that's where I can step in.

How, as a coach, do you help people? How is the strongest way to show up as a coach? By having ALL the answers?

On the contrary. It's by having NONE. The LESS you know about someone and their problems, or what they want to work on, the MORE you can help them. How is that?

By doing WHAT YOU DO. By asking questions. By being super curious. By being subjective. Coaching is all about bringing out from the person what's going on for THEM and helping THEM figure out the answers. The LESS you know, the more you have no agenda or idea of what NEEDS to happen. And if they don't know, and you don't either, the most powerful thing you can do as a coach is to tell them "I don't know." You DON'T have all the answers. That's the beauty of this.

YOU are not responsible for making anything happen with them or MAKING the results happen in their lives. You can only give them suggestions. You can co-create. But THEY have to make it happen.

THE COACHES' KEYS

So no, there's really nothing for them to sue you for, ever. It might be wise to get an LLC anyways, but speak to your lawyer about that, that's not my job here.

My job is just to help YOU empower YOURSELF, to realize those fears are just that. They are fears. Created by you. And they can be diffused by you.

Another point I'd like to make is, do you see how much of those fears are focused on you? What did we talk about already? If you are focused on you, you CAN'T help them. We need to FORGET about ourselves when being of service to someone. Not about how we look, how we are coming across, what are our credentials or certifications. In fact, ask ANYONE who is busy getting certifications or part of more and more programs why are they doing it? This is what you'll hear:

"Well, you have to have credentials."

"Because NOW people will know I am legitimate."

"Why would someone hire me because I decided I'm a coach without any schooling?"

All of these are self-centered and talking to their own insecurities. We are fundamentally misunderstanding peoples

~ 105 ~

REPHOEL WOLF

concern. IF someone asks you if you are certified or if you have credentials, it's because THEY are afraid of making changes in their lives, so any reason they can find to get out of it, they will.

If YOU are confident you can help them, they will feel that, and that will be enough for them.

Most coaches are getting certification for THEMSELVES to feel worthy. And you know what? It will never be enough. Because if the coach DOES NOT work on themselves and their own self-worth, no flimsy cheap paper or quick course will give them that boost.

I have even had coaches who have GOTTEN certified, when some other hot shot who was MORE certified questioned them about their certification and laughed at it! "You call THIS coaching certification? What you've learned was a joke!" And the coach was CRUSHED! All their hard earned credibility out the window!

But what is it really about? Is it about what you can show? Or is it about helping people? CAN you help people, yes or no? Are you in this field because you know you can change people's lives, yes or no? If you know you have what it takes to help

~ 106 ~

THE COACHES' KEYS

people, you don't need anything more than that.

IF someone challenges you and your background, challenge THEM right back!

Them: "What makes you certified to help me?"

Me: "I'm not. I just know that whoever I work with gets amazing results in their lives, but I am totally unqualified. If you want someone with really great credentials, I could totally refer you to them. Not sure if they will get you any results, but hey they sure are qualified!"

This business is really really all about the helping people. You can't feel dumb when you're all about helping the person in front of you. And you don't need anyone else to give you approbation for that.

CHAPTER 20

Serving NOW

Even after we get into this service mode, sometimes we may even still get caught up in our thinking too much. This is such a huge shift, it will take practice and mistakes and constant learning and tweaking. I myself only realized this after doing this for quite some time and didn't even realize it was something I was caught in, until my coach pointed it out to me. Which is WHY I have a coach. And why you, even though you're a coach, would benefit from having one too. Like we've already said, a coach is that outside pair of eyes who is helping you towards the same goal you want to reach, and who can see the things you

THE COACHES' KEYS

cannot because you are too close to it.

When I'm approaching the world, looking for problems to solve, looking for people to help, what if I see someone with a problem that I can help them with, but it's relatively simple?

What if I see someone, who really just needs a quick shift that will change things so dramatically, if they apply what I see. It could be a 15 minute conversation, how do I approach that? How do I approach someone to help them when they just need 15 minutes of my time (and their willingness to learn and apply)? What will I do after that? How do I go about extending this into other areas of their life which could have us working together for the next 3, 6, or even 12 months? I don't have that much to give them (that I can see right now that they need)!

I think this is a very valid question, but I wonder if you see within what I wrote the very ANSWER to this question. Well let me tell you, when I was IN this situation, I had no clue and I needed my coach to point that out to me. See, if anyone besides my coach, who is committed to helping me get to where I want to get, would hear my question, I think they would totally agree that it's a fair point. They might even say "They'll probably figure it out eventually. It's obviously not some big secret. When they do it long enough, they will figure out what works."

So that would be of ZERO service to me for someone to say that. I want to figure out how I may be missing something. BESIDES THE FACT that what they said makes no sense. When you are doing something long enough, if it's the WRONG thing, nothing will ever change. And people are really CONVINCED, even though it's not working, that they are doing the right thing. They are doing what they think everyone else is doing. But until they commit to investing on big change, nothing will change.

What my coach DID see here and maybe you saw it too, that my approach was all wrong. I had slipped out of the place of SERVING them, into the place of enrolling them as clients. I turned the focus away from THEM and brought it back to focusing on me. I'm worrying about what will I do AFTER this? How would this lead ME to a client? What if I don't have enough to help them with for 6 months? Me, me, me.

I'm sick of hearing about me. I want to serve THEM. I don't need to know what this might do for ME in the future, it might do NOTHING! (Even though it can't possibly do nothing

~ 110 ~

THE COACHES' KEYS

because when I am living a life of service, it automatically comes back to me. But even if it theoretically DOES do nothing.) I want to focus on who can I serve, RIGHT NOW in this present moment.

I don't go out into the world to serve people who MIGHT become a client one day. That's the wrong outlook. ESPECIALLY since I have no idea how my helping them with this one thing might sprout into a hundred new ideas, or make them want to look at all the other areas of their life with me. But besides for that, worrying about the future gets in the way of me completely serving people in this moment. And what we stand for is serving people. Helping people. Offering to help the problem we see right now, and who knows what will happen after that? That's not my business.

CHAPTER 21

Referrals

How can we get referrals? Where do referrals come from? How do we best utilize the referrals we already have? What ARE referrals?

Referrals are people that have been referred to us by someone who already knows us. If someone DOES NOT KNOW YOU, they WIL NOT REFER people to you. If someone DOES refer people to you without knowing you, you might want to think twice about how you're going to handle this person who has been referred to you.

You can't give your opinion about a restaurant you've never

THE COACHES' KEYS

been to. If you are still going to networking events (please stop), or you aren't (great choice) but remember back to when you did, you can imagine the scene. Imagine you're there and someone introduces himself as a restaurant owner and he's looking to spread the word about his restaurant, and he gives you his card and you part ways. That it. Quick exchange, you have my card I have your card, and we've accomplished nothing- I mean, we've done exactly what we think we're supposed to be doing at a networking event.

The next time a friend of yours asks you if you know any good restaurants, will you send them to this one just because you have this card? And if you WILL, will you tell them, go there, they're a good place and will take care of you? You can't POSSIBLY say that because you have no idea, unless you've gone there and EXPERIENCED it yourself!

The parable is simple. If someone is referring someone to you, they ALREADY know you, they've experienced you already, and they know this person would benefit from you as well. If they do NOT know you on a personal level, they are sending you someone that 1) they have no idea if it would be a

~ 113 ~

good fit for you, or even in your field altogether (!), because they have no firsthand experience with you. And 2) because they don't really care about this person they are sending to you. When we care about someone, we want them to be taken care of. We want to know they are in good hands. We want to be confident in where we tell them to go, so we better be doing our research.

When someone knows you and likes you and sends someone to you because they think you can help this person, what can YOU do for THEM? How can you leverage this referral partner so they will 1) keep sending people to you and so 2) you can build more and more referral partners?

Many people, in all industries, think that referral partners are a pay-off type of thing. When someone gives me a referral, I give them a gift. A certificate. Tickets to a game. A fruit basket. Maybe even a COMMISION!

This is very shallow. Almost greedy. It says "Thank you for sending me business. Thank you for sending me something that gives me money. Thank you for the money. Here is a present for the money you gave me."

THE COACHES' KEYS

EWW.

I don't like the feel of that at all. And they probably don't either.

SURE they like the gift. Sure it's nice to be appreciated. But you've made this exchange about an exchange of money. You've taken away the PURPOSE of what's happening here. You've taken the focus away from the fact that someone is being helped because of this exchange, and making it about a money trade. That's very shallow.

Why is someone referring someone to you? The relationships that are built on your refer-a-friend-and -make-money thing do not last. People refer people because they want to *have a part in changing this person's life for the better*! They KNOW you can help this person, so they send them to you because they WANT TO MAKE A DIFFERENCE.

So what do YOU do with that?

LET THEM KNOW THEY'VE MADE A DIFFERENCE.

Keep them posted.

Keep them in the loop.

Follow up with them.

Let them know what occurred because of their referral.

The deepest human craving is to make a difference in lives, to make a difference in the world. GIVE THEM THAT SATISFACTION.

If you DO NOT do this, if you just say "Thank you so much for the referral, here's a gift card", and you don't let them know what happens next, they WILL not keep referring people to you.

Why?

Because they do not know what happens when they DO send people to you! They don't know if the person is being taken care of. They don't know if you two ever started working together or if you even connected! They don't know if sending people to you is making a difference in anyone's life! So even if you thank them for a name, or gift them something for a client, there's nothing pushing them to keep sending people to you.

When I first learned about this, I'll agree, I thought it was extreme. BUT, and this is a very big BUT, I was a victim of experiencing this first hand.

I was literally minding my own business one day, when I got the following email. I got this email from a woman whose

THE COACHES' KEYS

coaching style I did not really connect with, whom I referred someone to who did not like MY coaching style. I connected them. This is the email I received:

Dear Rephoel,

I trust this finds you well and that you are enjoying the summer.

You kindly referred me to (name withheld) and I wanted to thank you very much for the referral.

I have just completed a 90 day program with her. In the process, I have created a new "coaching" format which I shall probably be using again.

I very much appreciate your thinking of me.

With all very best wishes,

(Name Withheld)

I was FLOORED. I was shocked. I was at a loss. I was appalled. I was so touched AND I had just learned about this! I was like "Who told her to do this?? How did she know the keys to the soul I just learned?"

THIS is what I wanted! I would have thought it "cute" if she sent me a gift card, but it would have had no meaning, and no impact. NOW I am happy with referring someone to her.

~ 117 ~

It was just a nice, thoughtful thing to do, and it's not like she has to pay herself off so she shouldn't feel bad that I gave her something and she didn't give me something. I have heard some people say that about their referral partners, they feel guilty for taking and not giving anything in return.

You CAN give in return. Give them the DIFFERENCE they have made. Touch them so deeply and keep them up to date with the going-ons. Fill them in, even if not the private details, but just that this person's life is being impacted because of their referral. And they WILL go out of their way to keep sending more people to you, because what a great, simple, and easy way to impact the world. By sending people in the right direction where they will receive help.

And the more you do that, the more partners you will build, because anytime someone refers someone to you in any slight way, you will be so appreciative *through* the difference they are making, that they will want to keep that up.

CHAPTER 22

Ditch Your Niche

Please read that title chapter however you work it out that those two words rhyme. I have heard many different ways of pronouncing the word 'Niche' so at this point, every way is valid, so let's read it in the way that rhymes with 'ditch'. OR you can pronounce 'ditch' wrong to make it rhyme with niche.

But either way, get rid of your niche. Stop limiting yourself. Stop locking yourself in. It's not helpful. You may THINK it is. But it is not.

Don't get me wrong. I'm sure there are specific types of people you connect with BETTER than others. Or certain areas you are more passionate about than others. Those could be your specialties.

But I've seen a lot of coaches get stuck in this area. They get either 1) hung up on WHAT their niche is or 2) get hung up that they don't KNOW what their niche is! I saw recently a coach post on FaceBook :

"What are your very best tips on choosing a coaching niche and target market? I've heard great tips on that and taken multiple great marketing trainings and spent so many months and countless hours journaling to figure out my niche which has really helped – yet it still just isn't quite as narrow and clear and "Yes! Jackpot!" as I'd like."

I messaged the woman and told her that I've done all that PLUS spent thousands of dollars on it, and I'd be happy to talk with her about it.

What would I say? "DITCH YOUR NICHE". You don't NEED one. WHY?

Well, why do coaches THINK they need a niche in the first place? The popular talk amongst certifications and trainings and 'build your niche formulas', is that if you don't have a niche than

THE COACHES' KEYS

1) no one will be able to find you, and 2) because you'll be just like every other coach out there. This can be one and the same, depends on how you look at it.

First of all, you AREN'T like every other coach out there because YOU are YOU. You bring to the world and to your clients only what YOU can bring to the world. No one else can do that. The reason you're even ALLOWED to be a coach is because there is still a need for you. What need is there for you when there are so many fantastic, amazing, and successful coaches out there? What need are you filling that is not being filled already?

YOU. You are filling the need for YOU in the world. If there was no need for you in the world, you wouldn't feel like you should be coaching. If coaching is your calling, and only YOU know if it is, then there is a need for you. And the people who need you to help them need YOU to help them. They need to hear YOUR voice. No one else's voice will talk to them or resonate with them.

So there's definitely a need for YOU, and you are NOT like any other coach in the world, regardless if you have a niche or

REPHOEL WOLF

not.

But secondly, about that which they say people will not be able to find you if you don't have a niche, please tell me really simply how HAVING a niche helps them find you better? As we've probably mentioned once before, you are not supposed to be sitting and WAITING for people to FIND you. Like that coach's website I saw (from her direct link, or else I would never have found it), that she has on her homepage a video that starts playing right away that says "I'm so happy you FOUND me!"

Isnt that just a dream come true, woman? They just FOUND you! Oh what a happy lucky day! Clients FINDING you as you sit comfortably by your desk, meditating and aligning your chakras and BOOM! Clients FIND you! I can't wait to see what happens next in that fairy tale! There MUST be a villain SOMEWHERE, there always is in the happiest of stories!

Back to the real world. There isn't some great big metaphorical "Find a service platform" where people come looking for a coach, but they can't find you because you are not holding a sign with their name.

(There actually IS a virtual platform where you can find a

service provider for almost anything you need, you just say what you're looking for and thousands of service providers battle it out to give you their best price and win you over. Do you think that a) you want that? And b) that your niche will do diddly squat for you there?)

They are NOT looking for you. In fact, I bet if you thought about it, the people you WANT to work with, they probably don't even KNOW they need help! You have to SHOW them!

If either way YOU have to find THEM, and they don't KNOW (yet) that they need you, what does limiting yourself to a niche help you?

It'll help you have an elevator pitch. Is that called finding your people? No. That's called hoping they will hear you and find YOU.

Maybe it's conversational to have a niche, so you can casually and suavely tell someone what you do if they ask? Why not just tell the person "I'm a coach"? And if they ask for more, offer to have a coaching conversation with THEM? Because there really is no way to describe what you do. It's an experiential service.

~ 123 ~

REPHOEL WOLF

STRANGER (at a dinner party): So what do you do?

ME: I'm a business coach.

STRANGER: Oh? What does that entail?

ME: I help people with their businesses and to make more money. I'd love to sit down and talk with you about it sometime, maybe I could help you as well!

STRANGER:

(option #1): No thanks, I'm good. Nice meeting you!

(option #2): Sure that sounds interesting!

Either way, I want to make sure all the conversations are USEFUL. If someone is just being chatty, I don't need to be chatty about my profession. So if they want, we can really talk about it. Or we can just move on to talking about what's for dessert.

You *know* which people you like working with most, or would like to work with. So go find them. You don't need to write down or tell anyone "What your niche is". It doesn't serve you in any way. And I've gone down that path; I'm not coming from being cheap and ignorant.

I have grasped onto the niche of my mentor, Steve

Chandler, "I'm A Life Coach. My Niche is anyone with a Life. And my target market is 7+Billion people." When I told him that is my niche as well, he asked that I should please make sure to save some people for him.

That's one of the reasons I love him so much.

I would like to end this chapter with a poem I wrote years ago about the power and uniqueness of YOU. It feels right over here.

Because YOU are YOU Thursday, April 28, 2016

Sometimes some feelings

can only make sense

because they are happening to YOU.

YOU, who has lived

everything that you have

and who has seen all you are

through the good and the bad

can fully grasp

how certain things just ARE

and can only be true to YOU.

REPHOEL WOLF

No amount of explanation

can justify you

in the way that you

justify yourself.

There are not enough hours

or days or years

to fully put into perspective

all that makes up YOU

for all the time that you spend

putting that into text

just builds up the next

set of time

that continues to make you

YOU.

For we are ever building

ever learning

ever growing

as beings we are

legions.

Fighters.

THE COACHES' KEYS

Explorers.

Developers.

Learners.

Warriors.

Lovers.

Magicians.

Kings.

And never sell yourself short

because you can't explain

why some things make sense

and others don't

because I honestly think

that each one of us can truthfully say

"Neither can I."

CHAPTER 23

How Quickly Can You Expect Results?

How long do you we have to wait for this 'giving people the experience first' thing to pay off? When can we confidently say 'this isn't working, I need a new job'? Like, it sounds like a nice theory, but is it actually practical? Well, how long after you plant a tomato plant seed do you decide that it's not growing and you should throw it out? A week? Two? Do you water it? Is it in a sunny spot? Have you ever grown a tomato plant? Do you know anything about growing tomatoes? There's a lot to look into before you decide you're the expert enough that knows it isn't working. That's where having a farmer who has been growing tomato plants constantly comes in, that could mentor you in this endeavor before you chuck out all your hard work and spend the rest of your days mocking anyone who tries growing tomatoes.

I have the most beautiful and wonderful letter that MY coach, David Schwendiman wrote in response to a woman. This woman wrote to Dave complaining about her partner, who was being coached by Dave, wasting his time as a coach. The woman wanted to know how long she had to patient with this coaching stuff and when can she force him to go get a 'real job.' With Dave's permission, I am publishing his response, as it it so good, it has to be shared with the world:

"The good news here is that we don't have to worry about you being patient. In fact no patience is necessary at all in this process! Total relief right?

The way to do this is to set an arbitrary deadline. A nice firm line in the sand for when he needs to make the exact amount of money through coaching that will qualify him as a success (I Googled that number just now but couldn't find a solid answer, sorry for the vagary) and then put tons of pressure on him to get there. I think you both have kids right? It's the same thing you want to do with them. Personally I have 2 children. I used to have 3, but when my middle child was 14 months old and still not walking... well, that was it. That was my line in the sand. Because I knew that if he wasn't walking by 14 months the chance of it ever happening was pretty minimal and I wasn't just going to wait around spending all my time and money on this child that was not living up to expectations. So straight to the orphanage with him.

Same thing in coaching. Sure it's a process; sure everyone has their own path to walk before they start seeing real results. Personally I made about [3 digit number goes here] in my first 6 months of coaching. Now granted I'd only spent [five digit number goes here] (plus a few thousand in travel expenses) during that time learning to be a coach which I believe equals a... 3.5% return on my initial investment. But don't worry, things got much better from there. Over the next 2 years I made a total of [5 digit number] in coaching fees while spending just an additional [5 digit + 4 digit + 4 digit + 4 digit= 5 digit] on my coach training, plus travel of course. Yielding me (if we exclude the travel) a

104% return on my investment! Then in my third year I brought in [6 digits] in coaching fees and spent [4 digits] on being coached. So a 2,566.67% (is that math right?) return.

I can't really speak to sustainability of such a career. My own wife was not happy with what I brought in my first, second OR third year coaching. I mean, sure it was $45,000 more than I'd ever made in my corporate job where I was climbing the corporate ladder faster than any of my colleagues, but still not quick enough. My total lack of success and inability to create a sustainable career coaching was a major part of what ended our marriage.

And if your partner is spending long hours on the phone each day trying to GET clients then I fear the problem may not be in the field he has chosen, but in how he is going about it. In my work with clients, both coaches and other professionals (like the custom home builder I worked with last year who made an additional $20,000,000 using our work together) I focus on SERVING people. Not helping them to GET clients. If you hear him doing that, the getting clients thing, Please knock the phone out of his hand and have him call me immediately.

REPHOEL WOLF

As for how long to let the FUN go on for? That's also a great question that I'm not sure I have a great answer for. I think it depends on how much success you can handle. I had a client (he will be a client again soon) who had ZERO FUN. He was a piano instructor, made great money for his field, and was a very SERIOUS individual. No fun was had when he was working. Or not working. He was very equal in his NO FUN policy. He came to me actually because he wanted to make more money and he wanted someone to show him the proper procedures to take that would make this happen. In short, how to "do it right". I totally messed this plan up for him. First I tricked him into paying me [4 digits] for 2 months of coaching. Then I pulled out my best material and hoodwinked him into spending [4 digits] for 6 months of coaching. During that time his income increased. As in went up over what he was making before. By $150,000. AND HE WAS MAD! He was mad because all I'd done was make him relax and play more during his working hours. To have more fun with his clients, his business and his family. No joke here (not that I was joking anywhere else in this email), he was actually upset with me because he couldn't figure out why just having fun and relaxing and truly serving those around him could make him so much money. But it did. And then this year he wants to

THE COACHES' KEYS

throw away more money on me so that he can bring home an additional (making it a total of $400,000 increase) $250,000 in 2018. Crazy stuff really. Especially since he made $50,000 in June alone. I mean on this track he's going to totally over shoot and blow away that $250,000 number. Boy is he going to be mad when that happens.

To boil it down in less coachy terms, here is what I see: your partner has more motivation, more drive than almost anyone else I've ever worked with. In fact, I have to try and slow him down at times he moves so fast. He's like a golfer running at the ball over and over taking swings. He has all the power and raw talent you could ever want in a coach. Our work is his finesse. It's like right now we are trying to start a fire by just pilling up leaves and sticks and leaving them in the sun. As we focus on him and his work, the way he helps people, as it gets more and more powerful, like putting a magnifying glass over the leaves to concentrate the sunlight... at first it can seem like nothing is happening. It's called "invisible progress" in the book Mastery. From the outside it looks like nothing is happening. And then BOOM! We have fire. But how long does it take? How long do we hold that magnifying glass over the leaves before we give up and just eat raw meat for dinner? I can't answer that. All I CAN tell you is that this process works. It works with

~ 133 ~

REPHOEL WOLF

everyone I've worked with who uses it.

Hope this helps. I know I feel better. Let me know if you have any more questions.

- Dave

THE COACHES' KEYS

About the Author

REPHOEL WOLF has read a long time ago, and has wondered ever since, how many people realize that the 'About the Author' section is ALSO written by the author himself, just like the rest of the book is? He is fascinated by this one sociably acceptable place to talk about oneself in third person.

REPHOEL lives in Chicago, IL with his wife and two adorable daughters. It is common for the author to state which cool pet they have, such as a zebra, but alas there will be no pets in his house. This is mostly his wife's doing.

After many many months and thousands of dollars learning the WRONG way to coach and get clients, Rephoel has found a path which not only combines the business side of coaching with the actual coaching part of coaching, he has found it has upped his quality of life in unexplainable ways.

He is passionate about helping people get unstuck, showing them where they might be stuck in the first place. And shawarma. Definitely shwarma.

~ 138 ~

Recommended Reading:

The Small Business Millionaire by Steve Chandler and Sam Beckford

37 Ways to Boost Your Coaching Practice by Steve Chandler

Fearless by Steve Chandler

The Go Giver by Bob Burg

The Go Giver Leader by Bob Burg

Getting Naked by Patrick Lencioni

Straight Line Leadership by Dusan Djukich

Selling From the Top of the Ladder by David Schwendiman

Wealth Warrior by Steve Chandler

Time Warrior by Steve Chandler

The Prosperous Coach by Steve Chandler and Rich Litvin

Made in the USA
Columbia, SC
04 April 2019